Drop That Chalk!

Drop That Chalk!

A Guide to Better Teaching at Universities and Colleges

Marie K. Iding
R. Murray Thomas

ROWMAN & LITTLEFIELD
Lanham • Boulder • New York • London

Published by Rowman & Littlefield
A wholly owned subsidiary of The Rowman & Littlefield Publishing Group, Inc.
4501 Forbes Boulevard, Suite 200, Lanham, Maryland 20706
www.rowman.com

Unit A, Whitacre Mews, 26-34 Stannary Street, London SE11 4AB

British Library Cataloguing in Publication Information Available

Library of Congress Cataloging-in-Publication Data

Names: Iding, Marie K., 1957- author. | Thomas, R. Murray (Robert Murray), 1921-2016 author.
Title: Drop that chalk! : a guide to better teaching at universities and colleges / Marie K. Iding, R. Murray Thomas.
Description: Lanham, Maryland : Rowman & Littlefield, 2017. | Includes bibliographical references and index.
Identifiers: LCCN 2016057914 (print) | LCCN 2017016032 (ebook) | ISBN 9781475823011 (electronic) | ISBN 9781475822991 (cloth : alk. paper) | ISBN 9781475823004 (pbk. : alk. paper)
Subjects: LCSH: College teaching—Methodology. | Effective teaching.
Classification: LCC LB2331 (ebook) | LCC LB2331 .I35 2017 (print) | DDC 378.1/25—dc23 LC record available at https://lccn.loc.gov/2016057914

∞ ™ The paper used in this publication meets the minimum requirements of American National Standard for Information Sciences Permanence of Paper for Printed Library Materials, ANSI/NISO Z39.48-1992.

Printed in the United States of America

Contents

Preface

This book is based on two university professors' more than sixty years of combined teaching experiences and their research in educational psychology, learning, and human development.

Marie Iding, a professor in educational psychology at the University of Hawai'i, has also taught in California, American Samoa, and Chuuk (formerly known as Truk) in the Federated States of Micronesia. She has delivered teaching and educational publishing–related workshops in Vietnam and Ecuador and has presented her education and technology-related research at many international conferences in such diverse venues as Scotland, Switzerland, Spain, Germany, Kenya, Jamaica, and South Africa. She has served as a visiting researcher in Bergen, Norway, and Copenhagen, Denmark.

R. Murray Thomas has taught in California, Hawai'i, Indonesia, Washington, and New York and has carried out research in American Samoa. His teaching and writing career began in the 1940s. He founded the international education program at the University of California, Santa Barbara, and was the first permanent dean of the school of education there. During his career, he has published sixty books as author, coauthor, or editor on a wide range of topics including education and human development.

He was Marie Iding's professor in the late 1980s and, during the writing of this book at age ninety-five, still enjoys interacting with former students and colleagues and reminiscing about a rich and exciting career.

During the authors' many years of working in higher education and mentoring graduate students and new faculty members, they appreciated the extensive preparation they received for teaching in higher education—a training based on their previous work as teachers and on their educational psychology research investigating aspects of teaching and learning. In comparing their training to the limited preparation most new professors experience, the authors decided to address this deficiency by providing others with the skills necessary to succeed as university and college instructors. Thus, Marie Iding designed a doctoral seminar, Introduction to University Teaching, for University of Hawai'i students, faculty, and staff members. The positive responses of students to the information she shared combined with the lack of preparing-to-teach texts for new university professors underscored the need for a book—this volume.

This book is also intended as a companion to *Becoming a Professor: A Guide to a Career in Higher Education* (Iding & Thomas, 2015). In that book, the authors describe the range of university or college teaching positions to which readers can aspire; ways to succeed at the application and interview process; methods for navigating the teaching, research, and service roles associated with faculty positions; along with techniques for handling politics and successfully carrying out the tenure and promotion processes. That volume briefly—in a single chapter—mentions some suggestions regarding teaching.

Because teaching is so central to most higher education positions and is so multifaceted, the authors recognized that it merits a separate book. And because the authors have found university teaching to be so rewarding in working with thousands of diverse students, sparking students' intellectual and personal growth and facilitating the authors' own growth and exposure to many points of view, they are energized to share what they have learned about university teaching with you.

Acknowledgments

Writing this book, we recognize with gratitude the many students and colleagues who learned with us and supported our growth as instructors in higher education. We thank these individuals. We particularly wish to thank the following people who contributed to the development of case studies, reviewed chapters, suggested titles, or made other contributions: George Harrison, Ron Heck, Brooke Janikowski, Jennifer Ninci, Adam Tanners, Malia Mallchok, Ravi Vatrapu, Teresa Arambula Greenfield, Ann Ito, Joe Swickard, and Paul McKimmy. We also wish to acknowledge Ravi Vatrapu and the Copenhagen Business School Computational Science Laboratory as well as the Center for Applied Information and Communication Technology, whose support enabled Marie Iding as visiting professor to work on chapter 7.

In Memoriam

During the final editing of this book, R. Murray Thomas passed away at age ninety-five. Murray led a rich and rewarding professional life from his early days as a crime reporter for *The Honolulu Star-Bulletin* and as a teacher at Kamehameha Schools in the 1940s. Later, at the University of California, Santa Barbara, he served as professor, dean of the Gevirtz Graduate School of Education, and director of the International Education Program. While an emeritus professor he added twenty books to his list of more than four hundred professional publications. As nonagenarian, he enjoyed interacting with colleagues and former students, writing books and poetry, and sketching. His memory, warmth, humor, kindness, generosity, writing, and artwork continue to inspire us—his readers, colleagues, friends, and family.

Introduction

This book is designed as a companion to our *Becoming a Professor: A Guide to a Career in Higher Education* (Iding & Thomas, 2015). This book focuses on the teaching role in higher education—a topic that merits a volume of its own—and was written especially for the following readers:

- Graduate students and others interested in pursuing careers in higher education and who wish to learn more about the teaching role in colleges and universities.
- New professors, instructors, and teaching assistants beginning their teaching careers.
- Experienced professors and instructors intending to incorporate new strategies, upgrade teaching techniques, better understand students, and generally improve their teaching.

Graduate students and others with advanced degrees might be assumed to have advanced knowledge about teaching in higher education. After all, compared to the general population, it could be presumed that they have completed more classes, experienced more instructors, and witnessed more instructional methods.

However, being a student is very different from planning a semester- or quarter-long course about a subject in which one is very familiar (or in some cases, not so familiar!). Determining which topics to focus on; setting instructional goals; meeting institutional, departmental, and professional objectives; choosing readings, textbooks, and other instructional materials; creating a syllabus; determining how to assess learning; determining instructional methods; and planning individual class sessions are all nontrivial and time-consuming tasks.

For most university instructors, preparation for teaching consists of observing professors and emulating their teaching methods—what we think of as the *osmosis* technique. Unfortunately, learning to teach via osmosis limits teaching methods to those that one has observed and can imitate along with trial and error efforts—not necessarily the most effective or efficient means of facilitating students' learning.

For a number of new instructors, serving as a teaching assistant (TA) is the hallmark of teaching preparation in graduate school. Although being a TA can be an improvement over no teaching experience—especially if the supervising professor or lead TA provides mentoring—one is still largely limited to osmosis: imitating and reproducing what one has observed.

Learning via osmosis does not provide the instructor with an updated knowledge base of educational psychology—the study of how students learn and how to teach effectively—or instructional planning and assessment of students' learning. Further, it does not provide instructors with tools to effectively match their own teaching and personality styles with strategies for improving teaching over time (i.e., instructional growth), nor does it expose instructors to innovative techniques that can facilitate students' learning, reducing trial-and-error efforts.

It is the goal of this book to bridge these gaps and provide answers to some of the most common questions facing new instructors:

- What should new instructors know about higher education students' characteristics that will help in designing effective learning experiences?
- What is the best way to develop a syllabus?
- What are instructional, departmental, and institutional objectives, and how can they be applied?
- What are the most effective research-based techniques for facilitating learning in different disciplines?
- What should new instructors know about research in higher education that can facilitate their expertise in teaching?
- What are useful strategies for developing courses online?
- How can students' learning be assessed? Which assessment techniques are most useful given different instructional purposes?
- How can instructors' teaching best be evaluated? What does research say about the utility of teaching evaluations? How can instructors most constructively use teaching evaluation results?

THIS BOOK'S STRUCTURE

The upcoming chapters are arranged to follow the general sequence of topics that the reader needs to consider when designing or teaching a new course or in redesigning a course that one wishes to update.

1. Chapter 1: Preparing to Teach provides expectations for teaching and suggestions for beginning instructors.
2. Chapter 2: Creating Instructional Objectives explains how to create objectives for your instruction.
3. Chapter 3: Instructional Techniques summarizes ways to provide effective instruction, including basic instructional techniques for neophytes who have little or no teaching experience. For experienced instructors, there are suggestions about how to improve instruction.
4. Chapter 4: Learning Materials and Technologies delineates various kinds of instructional materials and technologies, along with suggestions for how to integrate them into teaching.
5. Chapter 5: Assessing Students' Learning and Evaluating Instructors' Teaching distills major ideas about how to assess students' learning and how to judge the quality of one's own teaching.
6. Chapter 6: Characteristics of Your Students summarizes traits of students that will help you to understand them better, including the influence of their academic development level, ability, gender, ethnicity, culture, and more.
7. Chapter 7: Teaching Online describes major considerations in designing courses offered online.
8. Chapter 8: Creating and Maintaining a Positive and Constructive Environment describes ways to facilitate students' positive engagement in classes and techniques for dealing with challenging situations.
9. Chapter 9: University Teaching's Future describes trends likely to affect college teaching.

CONCLUSION

The dual purpose of this introduction has been (a) to suggest why the graduate student or newly hired professor will need to learn about *how* to teach despite many years of learning about the content in one's field and (b) to identify the themes covered in the chapters that follow. As readers progress through the book, they will recognize that the authors have incorporated many examples that illustrate issues commonly faced by higher education instructors.

Chapter One

Preparing to Teach

Assume that you have been hired or are contemplating being hired to teach in an institution of higher education, such as a two-year college, four-year college, university, technical institute, or the like. What things should you know at the outset if you are to be an effective instructor?

In this chapter, we focus on three of those things: (a) determining what your department expects of you, (b) preparing for your courses, and (c) planning lessons or deciding what you intend to do during class sessions. For the latter, we provide examples of how instructors might plan sessions and courses, given content requirements, students' backgrounds, instructors' specializations, and other considerations. In later chapters, we provide strategies for creating instructional objectives, descriptions of instructional techniques, and ways to assess students' learning.

WHAT YOUR DEPARTMENT EXPECTS OF YOU

It's important at the outset to discover what your academic department expects regarding the types of courses you will teach, your course load, your teaching style, and support services. You can seek this information by questioning the department chairperson and by speaking with other faculty members and students who serve as teaching assistants (TAs). If there is a faculty handbook, it may include information about such matters.

Types of Courses

As a new full-time instructor or professor, you will likely be assigned several new classes to teach. If you are fortunate, you might have taught or served as a TA in one or more of those courses before. Also, if you are lucky, you will be asked to teach a course in your own area of expertise.

Following are some questions and strategies to help you negotiate what you will teach, if there is any room for negotiation (which usually occurs during the interview or in actual negotiations for being hired, i.e., when you've been offered employment). If you are a graduate student or new TA, you are not likely to negotiate courses, but the following considerations should be helpful during future interviews for academic positions.

Are any teaching reductions offered for new faculty members? Often, institutions will provide teaching reductions for new faculty members in full-time, tenure-track positions, such as one course per semester or a couple of courses per year. The purpose of these reductions is generally to help you get started with your research agenda, particularly if a tenure clock is ticking, and also to help you develop as an instructor.

Although most departments hope for good teaching from new professors, experienced faculty members generally expect that you will become more polished as an instructor over time. They are aware that it takes time to develop expertise in teaching new courses and in first-time teaching, so if you have resources and opportunities such as course reductions, you may wish to take advantage of them.

Can you teach more than one section of the same course? In a typical research university, you might teach two or three courses per semester. It's helpful, especially in your first semester, to teach more than one section of the same course. That way, you can focus on developing, reading, and planning for that course.

As you teach one section, you learn which approaches are successful and should be duplicated and which approaches fall flat and can be discarded. You might find that the same approach works quite differently with two different groups of students. Then you need to analyze whether social differences existed between the two groups, such as daytime students and those in evening classes.

Your planning time will be reduced if you are teaching duplicate courses or sections. If you have any other choices in what you will teach, you might request a seminar in your own area of expertise. This allows you to capitalize on what you know and begin to develop a following of graduate students who might carry out research in your area.

Although you have been hired for a particular area of expertise, you typically will find your new institution quite different from your graduate program. When you were a graduate student, you likely worked with faculty members and other students who shared your academic interests. Perhaps your advisor and a few other faculty members and students worked together on different aspects of the same type of problem.

At your new institution, you might have been hired for exactly this specific kind of expertise because it is an area that is needed. Thus, you might find that no other faculty members share this particular area or emphasis and that you are expected to develop it on your own. This can have a range of implications for your teaching. Perhaps the courses you teach and the expertise you bring fill a large gap or need in the department. That means you will have to develop your teaching expertise rather quickly to fill a range of needs.

If you have never taught the courses that you are now expected to teach, you might take the following approaches:

- Request or obtain a course description. These are usually easy to obtain online on your department's Web site or in the course catalog.
- Ask the department chair for syllabi for the assigned course. You might ask for a mentor—a colleague who has effectively taught the course. You could observe one or two of this expert's class sessions and ask for examples of the kinds of activities or exercises that work especially well for the particular types of students. But if the course is a new one for the department, you may be obliged to search online to find syllabi for similar courses at other institutions.
- Obtain copies of any required guidelines or course objectives—either institutional or professional—that could be included in the syllabus you prepare for the class you will teach.
- Find out if there is a recommended textbook for the course. It is far easier, especially for introductory level courses, to use an existing textbook than to put together a set of readings on your own.
- Determine when book orders are due and to whom to submit them. In most instances, the department secretary will contact you. Most textbooks have to be ordered months in advance (not something easily done a week or two before classes start). Similarly, if you have particular requirements for your classes (software and other technologies, laboratory time), make sure that you know in advance how to reserve those items or whom to contact to arrange for them. Knowing who will help you and what procedures are required will go a long way in facilitating smooth and helpful interactions with staff members later.
- If you plan to hand out guide sheets or syllabi to your class members, who is expected to print the sheets: you, a teaching assistant, a secretary? These kinds of procedures can vary from department to department or from one institution to another. Find out if there are teaching assistants available to you and if there are special procedures for working with them.

CREATING A SYLLABUS

A syllabus is your contract with your students. It tells them what to expect of you and what will be expected of them. It also details how you will assess their learning. A good syllabus should contain the following items:

- The full title of the course, course number, and prerequisites (if any).
- A course description. This may be from the course catalog. However, you might want to augment it by adding a more complete description of your course as you will teach it.
- General course objectives. This may also be from the course catalog or from other departmental or discipline-specific guidelines. You might ask whether your department requires certain types of specific objectives on syllabi. (In chapter 2, we provide more details about designing instructional objectives.)
- Your name, information about how to contact you, including e-mail, office phone number, office address, and office hours. Some instructors provide their personal cell or home phone numbers. We generally consider that providing e-mail and office contact information should be sufficient and do not give out personal cell numbers except to graduate students with whom we work.
- A brief description of major assignments (papers, projects, presentations).
- A schedule that shows when assignments and readings are due, what topics will be covered, and when.
- Procedures for handling students' late or incomplete assignments.
- Your grading process and standards.
- Procedures for accommodating students with disabilities. This is usually a generic type of statement that is provided in most universities about resources that assist in accommodating students with disabilities and your willingness to be helpful in working to accommodate disabilities.
- A department or unit's conceptual framework or mission statement might be required or expected on syllabi.
- Relevant segments from your institution's conduct code or statement on academic integrity or ethics.
- Other college or university requirements, such as Title IX information. Title IX prohibits gender discrimination in educational or federally funded programs. Below is an example from the University of Hawai'i Office of Institutional Equity (2016):

> The University of Hawai'i is committed to providing a learning, working and living environment that promotes personal integrity, civility, and mutual respect and is free of all forms of sex discrimination and gender-based violence, including sexual assault, sexual harassment, gender-based harassment, domes-

tic violence, dating violence, and stalking. If you or someone you know experiences any of these, UHM has staff and resources on campus to support and assist you. Staff also can direct you to resources in the community. Here are some of your options:

If you wish to remain ANONYMOUS, speak with someone CONFIDENTIALLY, or would like to receive information and support in a CONFIDENTIAL setting, contact [List all Confidential Resources on your campus, i.e. student health center, counseling center or other resources designated as confidential by the Title IX Coordinator. Provide the name, location, phone number and other contact information as well as a brief description of services available and hours of operation].

If you wish to REPORT an incident of sex discrimination or gender-based violence including sexual assault, sex harassment, gender-based harassment, domestic violence, dating violence or stalking as well as receive information and support, contact [Insert the name(s) of the Title IX Coordinator(s), location(s), phone number(s) and other contact information, and office hours if such are restricted/limited].

As a member of the University faculty, I am required to immediately report any incident of sex discrimination or gender-based violence to the campus Title IX Coordinator. Although the Title IX Coordinator and I cannot guarantee confidentiality, you will still have options about how your case will be handled. My goal is to make sure you are aware of the range of options available to you and have access to the resources and support you need (p. 1–2).

Lesson Planning

A lesson plan describes what the instructor intends to do during a class session, unit, or sequence of sessions. A lesson plan can be as simple as an outline or list of activities or topics to be covered during a class session or as detailed as a fully developed set of lecture notes.

At the higher education level, lesson plans are not usually as detailed as the ones required for elementary and secondary teachers, yet when a new instructor actually starts planning a course, the necessity for carefully thought-out advance planning—and for overplanning, in some instances—becomes clear. When an instructor is uncertain about how long an activity might take or the extent to which students may be familiar with a topic, it's helpful to have alternate activities or methods for expanding upon instruction that's already planned.

The type of plan best suited for a class is determined by many factors, including course content and level, instructors' and students' backgrounds, programmatic requirements (i.e., things that need to be covered in the course), and nonacademic practicalities, such as number of students, access to labs, and other technologies.

EXAMPLES OF INSTRUCTIONAL PLANNING PROCESSES

Here we provide some examples of how a professor or new instructor might plan a class and describe factors that affect planning, including instructor's expertise, familiarity with content, and students' backgrounds and interests. How a particular class session fits in an overall course plan is also addressed. Our examples include courses from English literature, developmental psychology, biology of sex, and women's studies.

English Literature

A new assistant professor in an English department was asked to teach a course on the modern American short story while the full professor who regularly teaches the course was on sabbatical leave. Although the assistant professor's doctoral preparation included a general overview of modern American literature, the focus of her dissertation was on a contemporary South African writer.

To prepare for this new course, she requested and reviewed the syllabus developed by her colleague on sabbatical, and she reviewed other syllabi for similar courses that she found online. Ultimately, she selected the same short story anthology that the other professor previously used and decided to follow a similar schedule of topics and assignments.

On the first day of the course, she provided a general introduction and overview and reviewed the syllabus with the class, a group of thirty-two students. On the second day, her planning consisted of reviewing the two short stories that she had assigned as homework. She also reviewed biographies of the authors and several critical essays about the stories and read up on the historical context in which the stories were written.

Since the class also focused on developing students' essay writing and literary criticism skills, she began the class with a focused "freewrite" (an informal, five-minute writing activity) in which students wrote about their general reactions to the stories. For another several minutes, students shared their writing or, for those uncomfortable with sharing their actual writing, *about* their writing with a partner or in small groups.

She then gave a short lecture accompanied by PowerPoint slides that provided more historical context for the short stories. She transitioned to a discussion of literary analysis and explained how it differs from other kinds of writing that students might do in their other classes. She described literary devices, particularly focusing on characterization or tools by which authors develop characters.

She provided several examples of how characterization can be developed then asked the class in small groups of four or five students to come up with five examples of characterization from each story. She told the class they would have twenty minutes to complete this task. During this juncture, she walked around the room, sitting down with each group and adding to discussions or answering questions. After about fifteen minutes, the discussion appeared to wane, and she asked, "Does any group need a couple more minutes to finish their discussion?" Satisfied that they did not, she asked each group to report back, requesting that the person reporting back from each group be the one wearing the most color blue. She provided plenty of feedback to each respondent, praising accurate responses and encouraging elaborations.

As this discussion drew to a close, she asked the class for any remaining questions and reviewed the assignment for next week: two more short stories to be read and an essay to be written about how the authors achieved characterization in those stories.

Several things influenced her planning process. First, because she felt she did not have a strong background in this area of literature, she spent much more time reviewing background material about the author and the historical and social contexts of the writings. She prepared a short lecture but did not feel as confident about presenting a longer, more involved lecture filled with anecdotal information as she would about topics closer to her own area of expertise.

Second, she had not taught undergraduates at this level before and wanted to learn more about their backgrounds and thought processes regarding short stories and literary analysis. By eliciting their thoughts and reactions through freewriting and group-sharing activities, she was able to get a better idea about the level of their knowledge and how to better aim her instruction.

To increase their comfort about sharing and speaking in class, she encouraged them to work in small groups, to make sure that everyone, even the least talkative, had an opportunity to provide input. To dissuade naturally gregarious students from being the only ones speaking out in class, she asked for those "wearing the most color blue" to report back to the whole group (though she could have achieved the same effect by having students "count off" in groups and calling on the "number threes" or some other number). Further, she prevented downtime or off-topic discussion in the small groups by monitoring them, letting them know how much time they had left, and drawing the activity to a close as soon as there was a lull in group conversation. She was well aware that in this group of thirty-two students there would be time for four groups of five and two groups of six to report back to the whole class, although discussions might take longer with the larger groups than if they worked in smaller groups of two or three.

She continued her work toward developing positive affect and student confidence in speaking out in class and in sharing writing through her small group activities and by her positive, encouraging, and elaborating reactions to students' contributions in class. In doing so, she was beginning work toward her major goals: facilitating learning about the American short story and developing student writing.

Her lesson plan consisted of an outline of planned activities. Her materials consisted of her PowerPoint presentation and her preparation involved reviewing online materials and references in preparation for the class.

Developmental Psychology

An associate professor was teaching an introductory developmental psychology class to twenty students. The topic of an initial unit was Piaget's developmental theory. To determine students' level of familiarity with Piaget, he asked the class, "How many of you have heard of Piaget in other classes?" About half raised their hands. "What do you remember about him?" One student responded, "He had stages." The professor nodded. "Anyone else?" From the back a student said, "He had something to do with a dog and a bell." A few other students laughed a bit, but the professor acknowledged the student response by saying, "Thanks for trying, but you're thinking of Pavlov."

The professor moved on to provide a brief description about Piaget and introduced a few important terms: constructivism, assimilation, accommodation, and so on. He elected to project the terms via PowerPoint to minimize the time he would spend writing on the board, but since he knew the material well, he was equally comfortable using the board or PowerPoint. This was only a brief twenty-minute lecture, since he elected to show the forty-five minute film *Piaget on Piaget* in class, as the film was narrated by Piaget and illustrated children's performance in the actual developmental stages Piaget proposed. The professor reasoned that viewing the film would be far more memorable for students than reading yet another account of Piaget's stages in a textbook. After the film concluded, he encouraged students to discuss their reactions with partners, then students shared their reactions with the larger group.

In the remaining fifteen minutes of class, he introduced a cooperative activity called jigsaw (Aronson, 2000) for further work on Piaget's stages. He divided the class into groups of four, then told students that the present groups they were in were their "home groups."

Within their home groups, they counted off one through four, and these numbers indicated the "expert group" to which each student was assigned: each of the resulting groups focused on one of Piaget's four stages of development. Within these expert groups students learned about and discussed their respective Piagetian stage and prepared to teach their section to their home groups the following week, after they had done further research outside class. The professor carefully monitored their group planning in expert groups, making sure students understood key points and did not generate misconceptions.

His intention for the following week was to give expert groups a few minutes to wrap up their planning before each individual would return to his or her home group and present or teach information about their respective stages to the home group. The professor would lead a whole-class discussion about Piaget's stages and the theory in general. In their small groups, the students would evaluate Piaget's theory using "criteria for a good theory," which was presented on the first day of class.

Since he had taught this class numerous times before, his lesson plan consisted of a brief outline of activities; his materials included the video that was shown on his laptop and projected via audiovisual equipment in the classroom, and his PowerPoint presentation.

Courses in Biology of Sex and Women's Studies

For the courses Biology of Sex and Women and Health, a retired professor described her planning process. Since her background crosses biology and women's studies, the courses invariably covered topics that could be considered controversial (at least for some students). Rather than focusing on planning a single class session, she explained how she selected and approached topics that meshed with students' interests and maximally maintained their active involvement.

For Biology of Sex, a large, upper division lecture course of 180 to 200 students, the professor had a great deal of latitude in what would be covered. To determine major topics, she reviewed textbooks related to the course, attended to topics on current news outlets, and relied on ratings from her students from previous semesters regarding the topics that they considered to be most relevant to them from the course. To prepare students for topics to be covered, she explained on the first day of class that she would cover sensitive topics as honestly as possible with accurate scientific terms and that photos that could be interpreted as sensitive or explicit by some would be used.

To maintain a high level of student involvement in the lecture-oriented course, she employed several strategies. First, she gave six pop quizzes. Each was preceded by a short student review session in which they worked in pairs to prepare for the quiz (she described having students work in pairs throughout the semester a great deal). She used the quizzes and three to four exams as formative assessments helping her to determine what concepts students understood well and what they did not and which ones required further instruction.

As an example, she mentioned that early in teaching the course, she gave a technical lecture on hormones and puberty. In the quiz that followed, most of the students failed. As a result, she created a follow-up lecture in which the same material was presented via a very simple analogy in which the hormones are "memos" and the glands that produce them are likened to a hierarchy of workers in a tall office building who produce and send their memos "downstairs" to specific lower level workers telling them what to do. This method of teaching was so successful that all 100 students passed the subsequent quiz.

Despite the size of the course, she encouraged students' questions, called on students, and made an effort to learn their names. Additionally, she elicited concepts and principles from them. As an example, she mentioned a whole-class exercise on heredity with Punnett squares that involved giving the class "parental" characteristics and having them fill in the squares and answer out loud in chorus as they filled out the squares with the offspring's characteristics.

Sometimes, for a particularly complex concept, she would first tell students to put down their pencils and *not* take notes so that they could just listen to her and watch the accompanying PowerPoint presentation as she explained the whole concept. Then, after taking any questions students might have, she would go over the entire concept in detail again, this time with students taking notes.

In a smaller (fifteen to twenty student) seminar-style course, Women and Health, she described how focal topics were picked. She listed a number of topics that students might be interested in and had each student select and then rank his or her top five choices. From this she created a chart or matrix cross-referencing students' names with their top-ranked interests, ultimately assigning each student to two groups, each of which focused on one of their top-ranked choices; one topic was explored during the first half of the semester and the other during the second half of the semester.

For each of these topics she created a relevant problem-based learning scenario divided into four subtopics, with each person responsible for researching a different subtopic as the basis for their individual papers. The group members then combined all their individual research to develop, justify, and present to the rest of the class a group response to the problem using PowerPoint-enhanced presentations. Due to self-selection of topics related to individual interests, students were highly engaged in researching their topics.

For this instructor, the planning process was extensive, requiring that she be up-to-date with developments in the many areas related to reproductive biology and women's studies, as well as aware of her students' interests and concerns in these areas. She created PowerPoint presentations for her large lecture courses and quizzes and exams (which she graded herself to be attuned to students' levels of understanding). For her smaller seminar-style course, much of the planning took place early in the term, creating problem-based scenarios to address significant issues related to students' interests.

Throughout the remainder of the course, she often took a facilitative role, assisting students with their research processes.

CONCLUSION

In this chapter we suggested ways that newly appointed faculty members could (a) discover what their academic department expects of them as a teacher, (b) determine what they may wish to include in a syllabus for a course that they are assigned to teach, and (c) contemplate how individual professors might plan classes in several diverse fields.

The descriptions of planning processes touch upon only some of the many of the considerations that professors and instructors have as they plan courses to be as instructionally effective as possible. In the chapter that follows, we deal with designing instructional objectives, a central aspect of planning.

Chapter Two

Creating Instructional Objectives

Instructional objectives are your descriptions of the goals or purposes of your instruction—the outcomes or results you hope your students will achieve at the end of a unit or course of study. On most college or university syllabi, you'll find objectives listed somewhere near the course description or embedded in the course description. Generally, each course should have at least one or two clearly specified objectives that tie your instruction to expected student achievements or outcomes.

In education, there is a strong current emphasis on producing "measurable outcomes." Thus, by showing that students have learned something in your course, through your program, or at your institution, you are demonstrating the value of your program and of your course. This is especially critical during times of reduced funding and the rise of heavily marketed for-profit programs and associated student loan–related debt—factors that have provided the impetus for heavy scrutiny of higher education programs for employment-related program outcomes and other indicators of a course of study's value.

This chapter addresses aspects of objectives and outcomes and provides some suggestions that should help you to develop your own. First, we situate our discussion of objectives within an instructional planning approach—backward design (Wiggins & McTighe, 1998)—which will help you to match your instruction and assessments to your instructional goals.

BACKWARD DESIGN

We subscribe to the belief that the teaching process is usefully conceived as a process of backward design (Wiggins & McTighe, 1998), that is, as a sequence of three stages.

Stage 1: "Identify desired results. What should students know, understand, and be able to do? What is worthy of understanding? What enduring understandings are desired?" (Wiggins & McTighe, 1998, p. 9). Answering these questions enables you to identify learning outcomes or *instructional objectives.*

Stage 2: "Determine acceptable evidence. How will we know if students have achieved the desired results . . . ? What will we accept as evidence of student understanding and proficiency?" (Wiggins & McTighe, 1998, p. 12). In other words, how can students' mastery of the objectives be most effectively and accurately demonstrated? Answering these questions identifies the process of *evaluation*, *assessment*, or *appraisal* and, though at first glance it may seem counterintuitive, guides the actual instructional plan itself.

Stage 3: "Plan learning experiences and instruction" (Wiggins & McTighe, 1998, p. 13). Wiggins and McTighe (1998) provide questions to guide this stage of backward design:

- What enabling knowledge (facts, concepts, and principles) and skills (procedures) will students need to perform effectively and achieve desired results?
- What activities will equip students with the needed knowledge and skills?
- What will need to be taught and coached, and how should it best be taught, in light of performance goals?
- What materials and resources are best suited to accomplish these goals?
- Is the overall design coherent and effective? (p. 13)

What distinguishes this approach and makes it so useful is the emphasis on assessment and end products as central to course design, not the afterthoughts that many instructors and teachers typically may have conceptualized them as in the past. In the next section, we determine how one might find or create objectives for courses.

SOURCES OF OBJECTIVES

In higher education, sources of objectives can be institutional, program and departmental goals and objectives, college catalogs, textbooks, other instructors' courses, professional associations that provide accreditation and licensure for particular areas of study (e.g., nursing, teaching), and instructors' knowledge of their own subject matter.

For example, in nursing, the American Association of Colleges of Nursing (2008) provides a document entitled *The Essentials of Baccalaureate Education for Professional Nursing Practice* that delineates goals and objectives for such programs. They delineate nine classes of outcomes expected of graduates. Essential III is "Scholarship for evidence-based practice" (p. 3). As the document explains,

> The baccalaureate program prepares the graduate to:
>
> 1. Explain the interrelationships among theory, practice, and research.
> 2. Demonstrate an understanding of the basic elements of the research process and models for applying evidence to clinical practice.
> 3. Advocate for the protection of human subjects in the conduct of research.
> 4. Evaluate the credibility of sources of information, including but not limited to databases and Internet resources. (American Association of Colleges of Nursing, 2008, p. 16)

These are only four of the nine goals that exemplify this particular outcome. Examples of "sample content" follow and include such items as: "principles and models of evidence-based practice," "basic applied statistics," and "ethical conduct of research and scholarly work" (p. 17). Thus, programs can align objectives with these goals, and instructors can develop course objectives (if not already provided) in their own syllabi.

Other professional associations and organizations are likely to provide information about objectives and may also be good sources of information about teaching in your discipline. For example, the American Chemical Society has an entire section devoted to education and related resources on its Web site, www.acs.org/content/acs/en.html. So, too, does the American Economic Association, www.aeaweb.org/resources/teachers/student-guides.

Textbooks can provide sources of objectives, as each chapter of an introductory text generally contains an outline and objectives. However, these are generally more detailed—relating to each chapter—than the several that might be listed on a syllabus. Further, your course objectives may include the completion of a larger project—a research study, a literature review, a business plan—unlikely to be included in any textbook or set of books.

Your department or college is likely to have a series of courses designed into a sequence or set of requirements and electives. Related course descriptions contain goals that individual instructors are expected to incorporate into their courses and syllabi. Some may be quite general, such as, "Study of dance originating in North Africa and the Middle East. Topics may vary" or "Applications and techniques for problem solving in integral calculus." In these instances, you would be expected to determine an appropriate set of subtopics and course objectives that would fit your class.

Departmental colleagues or other instructors who have taught the course before can be good resources in providing examples of course objectives that they have successfully used in the past, as can syllabi for similar courses that you find online. However, it is useful to choose syllabi for courses taught by highly skilled and up-to-date instructors, and since there is such a current emphasis on effective assessment, outcomes, and objectives, it's best that you learn to develop objectives of your own. Strategies to help you do so follow.

BLOOM'S TAXONOMY

Over the past half century, a useful tool for identifying kinds of objectives to adopt for one's class has been the *Taxonomy of Educational Objectives* created by Benjamin Bloom and a group of other educators in 1956. The taxonomy is a scheme for classifying teaching/learning aims. Bloom's (1956) initial version was revised in 2001 (Anderson & Krathwohl, 2001).

In its present-day version, the taxonomy identifies three main learning domains: (a) *cognitive*, which concerns mental skills or knowledge, (b) *affective*, which focuses on emotions and attitudes, and (c) *psychomotor*, meaning physical skills. Within each domain, a series of behaviors is specified as learning objectives that students are expected to pursue. Instructors are able to select from among those aims the ones that will become the focus of their teaching in a particular course. Woolfolk (2016) describes the following six types of learning in the cognitive domain:

> *Remembering*: Remembering or recognizing something without necessarily understanding, using, or changing it.
> *Understanding*: Understanding the material being communicated without necessarily relating it to anything else.
> *Applying*: Using a general concept to solve a particular problem.
> *Analyzing*: Breaking something down into its parts.
> *Evaluating*: Judging the value of materials or methods as they might be applied in a particular situation.
> *Creating*: Creating something new by combining different ideas. (p. 537)

Although the kinds of objectives associated with the cognitive domain are generally the ones that relate best to most kinds of higher education instructional endeavors, many courses of study incorporate other kinds of learning—affective responses, such as to the arts and music, and psychomotor skills, such as those that involve dance and sports. Thus, below are Bloom's components in those areas.

The five components of the affective domain are: (a) *receiving* incoming information, (b) *responding* in some way, (c) *valuing* by demonstrating a preference for, (d) *organizing* by adopting a value, such as attending modern art gallery openings, and (e) *characterizing* by developing a strong commitment to, such as pursuing a degree in art.

The psychomotor domain includes: (a) perception (awareness of sensory cues), (b) set (readiness to act), (c) guided response (imitating to learn a skill), (d) mechanism (developing a degree of proficiency), (e) "complex overt response . . . or highly coordinated motor activities" (Gronlund, 2000, p. 116), (f) adaptation (capability of adapting responses to suit particular situations), and (g) origination (creating new types of movements).

To illustrate the application of the taxonomy, we can envision the way a professor might draw on the cognitive domain when planning the objectives for a college course titled Psychology of Development for teachers. The taxonomy's type of cognitive behavior represented by an objective is identified in parentheses following each objective.

One of the purposes of Psychology of Development is for students to:

1. Define the major characteristics of each of the major developmental theories, such as those of Piaget, Vygotsky, Erikson, and Case (*understanding*).
2. Apply Piaget's stages of cognitive development to an analysis of a child's tutoring session (*analyzing*).
3. Evaluate the above theories for their applicability in classroom teaching (*evaluating*).
4. Create a research proposal that builds upon one of the above theoretical perspectives for examining a developmental research question (*creating*).

THE FORM OF OBJECTIVES

A good resource for devising one's own instructional objectives is Gronlund's *How to Write and Use Instructional Objectives* (2000). In this section, we briefly describe some of the main ideas Gronlund espouses for creating objectives. As he explains, "Well-stated objectives clarify . . . expectations in terms of measurable or observable student behavior" (p. 4).

One method that Gronlund (2000) recommends is presenting a general objective and then "listing a *sample* of the specific types of student performance we are willing to accept as evidence of the attainment of that objective" (p. 10). The nursing example we cited earlier in the chapter would be an example of this.

Gronlund (2000) provides an example of a set of objectives for a project:

1. Conducts an experimental study.

    Devises appropriate experimental procedures.

    Devises controls for variables in the study.

Selects and manipulates needed equipment.

Uses measurement procedures correctly.

Analyzes and interprets the results.

Formulates valid conclusions. (p. 74).

You'll note that in the above example the objectives could be tied quite clearly to aspects of Bloom's (1956) taxonomy—a tool that Gronlund suggests may be of value to instructors. Gronlund cautions against being too precise in terms of measurable outcomes, such as by specifying a particular number of correct answers on a test in order to accomplish an outcome. He also advises against describing instructor behaviors rather than learning outcomes.

Finally, you'll note that all of these objectives are expressed with the use of action verbs. Thus, being familiar with these words can be helpful in constructing objectives of your own. Gronlund (2000) provides lists of action words that relate to aspects of Bloom's (1956) taxonomy.

Lower level cognitive outcomes—Recalling, translating, interpreting, estimating, comparing, classifying, applying

Higher level thinking skills—Identifying, analyzing, inferring, relating, formulating, generating, judging (p. 29)

For further guidance in developing instructional objectives, we recommend that you refer to Gronlund's *How to Write and Use Instructional Objectives* (2000). Should you or your department be interested in the larger process of designing program objectives and assessments, you might find such resources as University of Central Florida's *Program Assessment Handbook: Guidelines for Planning and Implementing Quality Enhancing Efforts* (2008) to be useful.

CONCLUSION

In this chapter, we proposed that the process of instructional design can best be conceptualized as that of backward design. We described sources of instructional objectives and explained how to produce them in written form.

Chapter Three

Instructional Techniques

The term *instructional techniques* is used to refer to various teaching methods designed to facilitate students' learning. The chapter does not address all varieties of instructional methods but rather focuses on the following most common types: (a) lectures, (b) class discussions, (c) student presentations and performances, (d) collaborative techniques, (e) internships and service learning, and (f) written assignments. Each type is discussed in terms of its typical form, its advantages, its disadvantages, and ways of enhancing the method's effectiveness.

We describe research regarding efficacy of each technique. Additionally, the following questions can be used to evaluate the techniques.

1. From the student's perspective, is the method efficient and effective, easily understood?
2. Does the technique motivate students to learn?
3. From the instructor's perspective, does the method seem efficient? In other words, given the amount of effort the instructor expends in preparation and instruction, does the "payoff" in terms of students' understanding and performance seem worthwhile?
4. Does the technique take into account the range of students' abilities, interests, and expertise? Put simply, is it useful for a wide range of students?
5. Is instruction aimed at the appropriate cognitive level? Below we explain this question further.

In other words, does the method elicit cognitive processing at the appropriate level of Bloom's taxonomy, given the level of material and ability of students? Bloom's original taxonomy (Bloom, Englehart, Frost, Hill & Krathwohl, 1956) indicates the level of cognitive processing or thinking involved using different instructional techniques (and is described in chapter 2).

The original taxonomy, which has facilitated instructional planning for years, has been revised to include the following six processes: remembering, understanding, applying, analyzing (breaking down a problem into manageable parts), evaluating, and creating (Anderson & Krathwohl, 2001). The taxonomy is helpful for considering whether your instructional goals and methods of assessment are appropriate for eliciting the kinds of cognitive processing you hope students will achieve.

LECTURES

Probably the best-known form of university teaching is the lecture—the professor at the front of the large lecture hall, leaning on a podium, delivering information for an hour, perhaps longer, and students scribbling notes—a familiar scene for most. However, the lecture approach has been decried in some educational circles as "old fashioned 'chalk and talk,' as mere information transmission, and the lecturer as an antiquated 'sage on the stage'—in need of replacement by an interactive, constructivist 'guide on the side' (King, 1993)" (Friesen, 2011, p. 95).

Despite this shift, we take a pragmatic view most closely aligned with Woolfolk's (2016) perspective on direct instruction (Rosenshine & Stevens, 1986), including instructors' explanations or lectures. As Woolfolk (2016) states, "Every subject, even college English or chemistry, requires some direct instruction" (p. 542).

As Woolfolk explains, some of the earlier research indicating students did not learn as well from lectures was done with students in large groups, not incorporating techniques that would actively engage students during instruction. Furthermore, despite the criticisms of lectures and direct instruction, we do not anticipate that the lecture will suffer its demise any time soon—witness the popularity of PowerPoint presentations and TED talks. (For those who are interested in learning some of the TED speakers' techniques, the book *Talk Like TED* [Gallo, 2014] is an interesting read.) Instead, the lecture will be enhanced by new technologies and methods of actively engaging students.

Friesen (2011) also takes issue with these disparaging perspectives on lectures. Using historical analysis, he traces the history of the lecture from "cultural preservation," which in medieval times involved reading texts before an audience. At that time the text (frequently the Bible) was considered to be the authority. According to his analysis, the transition to a reading accompanied by an explanation, or "lecture as hermeneutic event," to lecture as "illusion" where the speaker creates and interacts with the audience in what appears to be extemporaneous fashion took place and is now synonymous with what we consider to be contemporary lecture style (currently synonymous with the TED lecture).

As Friesen (2011) explains,

> The lecture has been much maligned as a pedagogical form, yet it persists and even flourishes today in the form of podcasts, the TED talk, and the "smart" lecture hall. . . . [He describes] the lecture as pedagogical genre . . . as bridging oral communication with writing and newer media technologies, rather than as being superseded by newer electronic and digital forms. The result is a remarkably adaptable and robust genre that combines textual and ephemeral event, and that is capable of addressing a range of different demands and circumstances, both practical and epistemological. (p. 95)

What is your role in this? Some people are gifted lecturers and speakers. Richard Feynman, the renowned physicist, comes to mind, or Martin Luther King Jr., as well as many of the TED speakers. Many, perhaps most, however, are not naturally gifted lecturers and have to work hard at developing this skill. And whether you plan to teach with a lecture style or using other instructional techniques, lecturing skills are important for presenting your research and giving a "job talk" so that you can get hired for that university teaching position. These skills are also useful for interacting with other faculty members and instructors when serving on teaching-related committees.

Advantages of Lectures

As Woolfolk (2016) contends, direct instruction, also known as lectures, are useful for "basic skills" or "clearly structured knowledge and essential skills, such as science facts, mathematics computations" (p. 540) and similar topics like foreign language vocabulary. Some information can be perhaps ideally conveyed by lecture: your latest research findings, for example. A new way of seeing research or theory development in a field or a general overview of major concepts or a problem-solving strategy might all be taught using lectures, especially if combined with other methods. Another advantage can be reusing or simply updating lectures from year to year.

Disadvantages of Lectures

Lectures require a great deal of advance planning time on the part of instructors. And if the instructor does not build in a great deal of interaction with students to formatively assess their understanding (or a pretest), there is a chance that the lecture will be aimed at the wrong level of understanding. If an area requires more elucidation by the instructor than was planned, the lecture can go offtrack—a potentially challenging scenario for a newbie. A further disadvantage is the difficulty of maintaining students' attention throughout the entire lecture. Finally, if students are taking notes, those who are slower due to language, disability, or sheer note-taking speed will fall behind.

Evaluation of Lectures

Keeping in mind the questions or considerations we raised at the beginning of the chapter, we rate lectures overall as efficient from the instructor's perspective in terms of conveying a great deal of information in a short amount of time (although inefficient in terms of large amounts of preparatory time invested in each one). However, unless the instructor builds in the kinds of formative interactions that ensure students understand, rating on students' understanding and motivation will be not so high.

Lectures do not tend to be tailored to many levels of student understanding, so they would be rated lower there as well. Finally, in considering the cognitive level known as Bloom's taxonomy (Bloom, Englehart, Frost, Hill & Krathwohl, 1956), most lectures, particularly those involving introductory material, would be aimed at the understanding, comprehending, and applying levels.

Improving Your Lectures

Keep in mind that if you lecture—or are expected to lecture—there are ways to increase student involvement and maintain their attention:

1. Start your lecture by finding a way to truly capture students' attention. Ask a thought-provoking question. Make a controversial claim. Raise an issue discussed in current media. Share an anecdote, then lead into a more general discussion that relates to the content of your lecture. If you are a science instructor, do a demonstration. In a chapter devoted to lecturing, Morton (2009) has several useful suggestions, including, "Describe a problem or scenario that is of relevance to the topic, then go on to outline how the lecture will consider this" (p. 60). Explain the objectives of the lecture and what students will learn during the session. Further, she recommends telling students why you are interested in this topic or how it relates to your own research.

2. Maintain interest by interspersing your lecture with opportunities for student involvement. Ask questions. If you are teaching a large group of students, ask how many support a particular point of view. How many support an alternative perspective? Ask for a show of hands. Stop and ask students to discuss a point with someone sitting next to them. Have one or two students report back to the class. Ask rhetorical questions. Use the Socratic method to prompt your students to think through to the next point.

3. Periodically check for audience understanding. If you are not technologically inclined, you can ask for a show of hands to indicate how many understand or agree or disagree with a point. Use simple questions like: How many understand so far? How many would like further explanation? For technology enthusiasts, you might use "clickers" or other forms of technological responses (i.e., audience response or student response systems). If you'd like to have written responses, make use of what Svinicki and McKeachie (2014) and Wilson (1986) call the "minute paper." Have students write about what they understand or don't understand for one to three minutes. Call on one or two students to share their comments. Collect the responses. As you gain experience teaching, you can tell by nonverbal indicators (e.g., facial expressions and general interest) whether your audience is with you or left in the dust.

4. Do not use allusions that your audience or the majority of your audience is likely to be unfamiliar with (Thomas & Thomas, 2008). In other words, keep in mind the general level of your audience. As Thomas and Thomas explain, the best material for a lecture is that which matches your audience's knowledge level; otherwise, those who know the material will be bored and those who are unfamiliar with their own subject matter will be lost.

5. Use advance organizers (Woolfolk, 2016). Advance organizers involve activating appropriate "schemas" or related information in students' memories. According to Mayer (1984), they can involve reminding students of something else that is relevant (e.g., a similar novel or a similar historic conflict) or, in the case of completely new material, provide a preview, overview, or presentation of new material that students will need to understand the lecture. In an English literature class, an instructor might define characterization, then describe actual examples.

6. Use examples (Woolfolk, 2016) and analogies. These are wonderful ways to tie abstract concepts to familiar and easily-to-visualize concepts that students already know. If you are using analogies, make sure that the presumed-familiar objects or concepts really are familiar to students and explain the shortcomings of any analogy (Iding, 1997).

7. "Anticipate and plan for difficult parts in the lesson" (Woolfolk, 2016, p. 544). Think back to your experience as a student or if you are an experienced instructor determine with which areas students are likely to have difficulty. Focus on them in your planning.

8. "Make clear connections by using explanatory links such as *because*, *if-then*, or *therefore*" (Woolfolk, 2016, p. 544). Explanatory links are helpful for creating coherence within the lecture.

9. "Signal transitions from one major topic to another with phrases" (Woolfolk, 2016, p. 544). Clearly stated transitions reinforce structure for your lecture. Statements like "next, we'll discuss . . . " or "in summary" are examples of signals of transitions.

10. Use techniques employed by good speakers. Do not read directly (or appear to read) from your lecture notes. Make notes that are short phrases, rather than complete sentences that you will be tempted to read. Look up at the audience. If you are using PowerPoint or other presentation software make sure that you are facing your audience, perhaps with the computer that you're using to switch slides in front of you. If you're using a remote control device to switch slides, look at your audience as much as possible and ascertain that you're not blocking their view of the screen.

If you're teaching mathematics or a topic that involves extensive blackboard or whiteboard use, make sure that you face students as much as possible. The first author remembers working with a teaching assistant (TA) who had been videotaped while teaching. The TA faced the board most of the time and talked nonstop, almost as if to prevent anyone from saying something or interrupting in any way. When asked why he never paused at all, he answered quite frankly, "I'm afraid that somebody will ask me a question and I won't know the answer!" (If you are ever in a situation like this, you might respond, "That's a good question. Let's see if we can find the answer.")

11. To improve your speaking style, vary your pitch and intonation and arrange to be videotaped while lecturing. We have all experienced tedious, monotonous speakers, and each of us has probably vowed to not be that person. Then one day we suddenly look out into a yawning sea of faces, several partially blocked by laptop screens and other class members surreptitiously playing with cell phones. That's when we recognize the need for improvement.

If you are naturally an introverted or soft-spoken person, your lecture style could be interpreted as unenthusiastic. A useful solution for that problem is to be videotaped. For some instructors, this might be a somewhat painful experience, at least at first. Get past "Do I really sound like *that*?" or "Why do I keep gesticulating *that* way?" and focus on your strengths. Perhaps you are well organized or really do sound as if you know what you are talking about.

But perhaps you do tend to speak in a bit of a monotone. What are some ways to improve? Turn the situation around so that you are not the center of attention. Ask questions. Vary your tone. Talk about something that really enthuses you and relates to your lecture topic. Sometimes merely speaking more loudly helps. Notice times when you are most engaging and enthusiastic, and try to incorporate whatever elements that prompted that enthusiasm into your lectures. Capitalize on your strengths because you *do* have them.

12. Incorporate multimedia. Pictures, video clips, and visual models can generate interest as well as make your content more memorable. One of the authors never forgot an oceanography professor more than twenty years ago who showed "home videos" of footage he had taken from Alvin, a submer-

sible (submarine) that had been used to explore hydrothermal vents in the ocean floor. We have since found that popular shared media sites have wonderful examples of classic psychology experiments and brief clips of luminaries in the field. In many instances, students are far more likely to remember a video clip of an important researcher or experiment than a verbal description that they read about in a textbook.

13. "Know how to use the presentation equipment" (Morton, 2009, p. 60). Even if you know how to use the equipment at home or in your office, the setup at the lecture hall might be different. The first author attends numerous conferences related to computers, educational technology, and learning. Invariably and ironically, at least one speaker always experiences some technology glitch. This results in wasted time and even sometimes a wasted presentation.

Go to the lecture hall beforehand (even on another day). Enlist the aid of a technology assistant (often a knowledgeable student because—let's face it—our students are often more technologically adept than we are). Practice. Also, be prepared with alternatives (e.g., handouts) in case the technology fails. We have taught in conditions with power outages during evening classes, or no more technology than a piece of chalk and a blackboard and an eraser consisting of a student's rubber sandal. Thinking through possible outcomes and solutions in worst-case technology-failure scenarios will prevent your whole session from going awry and can sometimes be fun.

14. Use resources—books, online resources, clubs like Toastmasters, which focus on public speaking. Try various techniques. For example, Gallo (2014) analyzed TED talks and determined that the most effective ones told a story (or touched the emotions in some way), presented new information, and were memorable or presented content in unforgettable ways. An example of the latter was Bill Gates setting a jar of mosquitos free in the audience. (Note: the mosquitos were not malarial and we do not recommend your emulating this approach.)

CLASS DISCUSSIONS

Here we differentiate whole-class discussions from small-group discussions, which are covered under "cooperation and collaboration." Whole-class discussions focus on the whole class's involvement in a particular discussion topic. These can include debates and other variations.

Advantages of Discussions

Discussions, if properly planned, moderated, and executed, can provide an effective way of involving students. The use of discussions can facilitate students' development of reasonable personal mental representations of the subject matter being discussed. Discussions can be highly motivating, especially if a controversial topic is the focus of the discussion.

Discussions can help students to do the following:

- Solidify or develop points of view regarding particular issues (e.g., ethical questions, treatment issues for students in social work, approaches to legal or business questions).
- Articulate ideas or proposed solutions to problems.
- Learn about others' points of view.
- Create ways to persuasively argue about major points.
- Practice speaking and reasoning extemporaneously in disciplinarily appropriate language.
- Overcome fears of public speaking by making smaller, confidence-boosting oral contributions than those that they would make in full-length oral presentations.

Disadvantages of Discussions

If not well-planned and moderated, discussions can fall flat. Consider the following scenarios.

A lecturer asks students to discuss the causes of the Civil War. Students are uncertain about what aspects of causes they are supposed to discuss and what the final outcome is supposed to be.

An instructor asks students to discuss the role of women in today's workforce. Since students know that the underlying goal is to support feminism, not much discussion is achieved.

An instructor poses a discussion topic around the Euro that seems of interest to a class in international economics. One or two students raise their hands to contribute. These are the same students who always respond to the instructor's questions. The rest of the students do not participate.

A professor poses an interesting discussion question involving a current event, but the whole discussion quickly goes off topic and does not return to the main topic.

An instructor poses an emotionally "hot" topic as a discussion that touches upon a sensitive issue related to gender, sexuality, culture, or ethnicity. Tempers flare, and several students seem just short of a shouting match.

What isn't working in the previous scenarios? Sometimes instructors pose questions that don't make for good discussions, such as questions that aren't open ended and for which there is only a single right answer. If the instructor has a particular position in mind that students can easily detect, a true discussion is likely to fail.

It is also possible that an instructor can pose an interesting discussion question or topic, but if students haven't been given the opportunity to do readings or research beforehand, they might not feel that they can make meaningful contributions to the topic.

In summary, discussions or debate-like activities are unlikely to succeed if students have little investment or interest in the topics under question, if the outcomes seem predetermined or destined to align with an instructor's underlying agenda, if students do not have sufficient opportunity to research or prepare their positions, or if a few outspoken students dominate the entire activity.

Evaluating Discussions

We assume that for some content, the use of discussion is an effective teaching method. And even if used frequently, discussions may be used in conjunction with other methods. If we consider the question that we proposed early in the chapter for evaluating instructional techniques, we find that discussions can rate highly on motivation. Depending upon how well discussions are planned, they can also rate highly on engaging a range of students, especially if students with differing perspectives or those from different backgrounds are active participants. Discussions can also rate highly on cognitive level, if the topic and questions posed are intellectually demanding.

However, discussions can sometimes go off track or focus on specific aspects of a topic at the expense of others, causing us to rate them less highly on efficiency. Further, although putting a discussion together can involve less of the instructor's preparation time, discussions can often involve spending more energy than one expects in intervening to bring discussions back to main topics, correcting misconceptions, and subsequent teaching to follow up on topics that should be researched further or were not sufficiently addressed by the discussion.

Clearly, discussions can be effective, depending upon the type of content and the instructor's goals, but discussions are not ubiquitously effective teaching methods. For example, contrast a lesson for undergraduates on the basic physiology of different types of muscles to a doctoral seminar addressing a similar topic. For the undergraduates, the topic would be minimally effective if taught via discussions. In contrast, for doctoral students developing research on related topics, discussions of recent research they are reading would be highly appropriate and effective.

Improving Discussions

If used effectively, discussions can stimulate critical thinking and inspire students' research. Here are some suggestions for improving discussions:

1. Use genuine open-ended questions. Real questions for which there may be no "right" or "wrong" answers, but only better or less well-reasoned ones

are more likely to generate good discussions. "How can the U.S. prison system be reformed to decrease recidivism?" might be one of those questions.

We feel that some of our best discussions in classes we have taught have been those in response to such open-ended questions. However, an instructor also has to be comfortable not knowing all of the answers in his or her discipline, because discussions in response to genuine questions can lead in directions in which the instructor might have limited expertise or in areas in which the class and instructor might propose to do further research.

2. Ask precise questions. Well-crafted discussion questions like well-crafted essay questions give students ideas of what the outcomes (in contrast to the specific answers) might be. For example, "Discuss the major causes of the 1960s civil rights movement in the United States. Delineate four or five causes that predominated." Or "Did the occupy movement that emerged internationally in 2011 parallel the civil rights movement of the 1960s? Describe three similarities and three differences."

3. Give students time to prepare for discussions. Discussions are much more effective when students have sufficient time to prepare for them. Announcing that the class will have a discussion about a particular topic at a future class session allows students to contemplate the topic as they complete their readings in preparation for class, and they can do further research if necessary. Clearly, a planned discussion can often be more effective than an extemporaneous one. Asking or assigning students to take sides on an issue and prepare in small groups in advance of doing readings can be helpful as well.

4. Actively moderate discussions. Discussions should be well moderated. If a discussion goes off topic, the instructor needs to steer it back to the original topic, perhaps by saying something like, "We seem to have gotten off track. Let's move back to the main question."

Some instructors may be uncomfortable doing this, feeling that they are stifling their students' ideas, but some guidance may be necessary if the original topic is to be addressed. Sometimes discussions segue into interesting asides that might be worth pursuing. Here the instructor needs to determine whether the digression is worth pursuing and for how long.

5. Ensure widespread or unanimous participation. Instructors need tactics for encouraging responses from students other than those who can always be counted on to volunteer answers. So an instructor might say, "Let's hear from someone who hasn't shared an opinion so far." "Let's hear from someone on the other side of the room" (or from the back row). If only a couple of students repeatedly respond and dominate discussions, the instructor might structure the activity so that each student might respond only a predetermined number of times (perhaps twice or three times) before others make their contributions.

6. Use adequate wait time. Instructors need to make use of the concept of "wait time," an idea that most K–12 teachers learn about (Slavin, 2011a). Specifically, instructors need to give students enough time after they ask a question to think about and articulate an answer before they can be expected to respond. Counting for about three seconds may help, although much longer may be of negligible use in terms of helping university students, especially if you are calling on them individually (Duell, 1994). However, some instructors we have observed are so eager to move on to the next point that they don't give students enough time to answer. This is particularly true of people leading discussions in college classes for the first time.

7. Allow students to explore answers with partners or neighbors prior to a whole-class discussion. It's often clear that a good, thought-provoking question has been asked, but sometimes students appear to be deep in thought and not ready to answer in front of the whole class. In these instances, ask students to talk to someone sitting next to them for a few minutes or to discuss the question in groups of three. Then ask for a few students to report back to the whole class.

8. Set ground rules for discussions, particularly for hot topics. Some topics can be emotional, such as those related to gender, sexuality, ethnicity, and religion. Some instructors, especially those used to teaching courses in those areas, can handle these topics deftly. Others might be less comfortable. In these instances, it's helpful to set up some ground rules, perhaps letting students know about them at the beginning of the discussion. For example, you can caution class members to listen and respect other participants' perspectives, and no one should insult anyone else. Sometimes the instructor needs to intervene, asking participants to step back before the discussion gets "out of line" or "too hot."

PRESENTATIONS AND PERFORMANCES

Some disciplines center around performance—the arts and music, for example. Others can employ student presentations and performances as ways to showcase student learning, enable students to teach each other, and allow students to practice speaking and presentation skills that can be central to career success. Examples can include presenting the results of research projects, presenting posters similar to those found at research conferences, performing musical pieces, or acting out scenes from plays.

Advantages of Presentations and Performances

Advantages can include high levels of student involvement and motivation, especially if they are given some latitude in selecting their own topics. Furthermore, students can learn more—at least about the topic that their presentation focuses on—if they are presenting or performing. An advantage for instructors can be that you may need to prepare for that class session less than if you were planning a lecture, but you will still need to carefully monitor students' planning and preparations.

Disadvantages of Presentations and Performances

Disadvantages can include less learning about topics taught by other students, especially if students have misconceptions that you need to monitor and correct. Students can digress from major information you want them to cover regarding particular topics, and of course, the quality of presentations can vary.

Evaluating Student Presentations and Performances

When we consider the considerations and criteria we proposed earlier, we find that student presentations and performances can rate less consistently in certain areas. For example, motivation can be very high if students are truly interested in the topics they have selected and are presenting or performing.

Motivation, attention, and interest can be lower for others' performances or presentations if students determine that the information to be learned from colleagues is not credibly presented or unnecessary to know for earning their own grades. Likewise, ratings on efficiency can vary.

If an instructor is clear about what she or he expects from presentations and what factors will be considered in grading, presentations and performances could be rated more highly on effectiveness in terms of the amount of learning that takes place. Frequently, however, instructors are less clear about expectations, resulting in presentations that can range in quality from excellent to unrehearsed and superficial. Thus, effectiveness can be quite high for students who prepare well, do research, and rehearse, and less so for those who do not. Cognitive level would be high, especially for those doing the presenting.

Finally, presentations and performances rate highly on taking into account students' varying interests and backgrounds and can create fewer demands on instructors' preparation time than some of the other techniques, depending upon how involved the instructor is with students' planning and preparations.

Improving Presentations and Performances

Suggestions for improving student presentations and performances include the following:

1. Be clear about expectations. Do you expect students to present material that's in the assigned textbook or to do outside research on particular topics?

If outside research is required, how will you ensure that they select credible outside information sources? Are they expected to lecture or lead discussions? How will they ensure other students' active involvement and participation?

2. Make sure that students practice or rehearse beforehand, even if you provide some class time for students to do so in small groups (although very likely not in front of the whole class). The whole class will be aware of (and likely disappointed by) extemporaneous presentations.

3. Monitor students' preparations. For example, ask for a brief outline in advance and confer with students or groups of students presenting similar topics. This gives you an idea about what will be presented in case you need to intervene if the topic seems unrelated to your instructional goals, involves misconceptions that need to be corrected, or if you find that students with similar topics need to confer with each other to prevent duplication of presented information.

Also, if students are working in groups, find out what each student is responsible for to ensure equivalent individual contributions at both preparation and presentation phases.

4. Be strict about time limits, particularly when students are presenting in groups. A solution is having an assertive student or TA monitoring the time allocated for each presentation and notifying presenters when the last few minutes have arrived. This prevents very enthusiastic, highly verbal students from taking time away from the others' presentations that follow.

5. Be clear about scoring. Using a rubric or scoring system that is distributed beforehand will help ensure that grading is fair and make your expectations clear to students.

6. Provide students with some freedom to select their own topics. They are likely to provide better presentations and more thoroughly research topics for which they have genuine enthusiasm and passion.

7. If students are using technology, such as presentation software that involves hooking laptops to projectors, make sure they know how to use the technology and that they come to class early and set it up in advance. If the expectation is set that you or your teaching assistant will be responsible for making their technology work, you might find yourself wasting valuable instructional time troubleshooting technology problems.

8. Decide whether to have students score or provide feedback about each other. In some instances, student evaluations of their colleagues' teaching are factored into grades. We prefer to have students provide written feedback to presenters, but these are not for the instructor. That way, students are more likely to provide useful feedback to other students. We also encourage students to address two areas—strengths of the presentation and suggestions for improvement—and we emphasize that this feedback be provided in a positive, constructive, collegial context. If students are presenting in a group, we

request that group members write brief reflection papers about their presentation to be submitted to the instructor. These papers can also help in assigning grades, as students will reflect on how their preparations succeeded and whether all class members consistently participated.

COLLABORATION AND COOPERATION

Collaboration involves students working together and can involve working in pairs or in large groups—tutoring, presenting, researching, problem solving. Collaboration is a broader term than cooperation. Cooperation often implies student collaboration but with a shared reward structure (Johnson & Johnson, 1985), such as all members of a group working on a project being given the same grade. Throughout the rest of this section, we employ the broader term, collaboration.

Advantages of Collaboration

Collaborative techniques can be valuable for tutoring students who do not understand a topic, for enabling students to research and develop areas of interest beyond the basic class material, and for allowing students to develop communication strategies about the material with each other. Topics that work well are also ones for which students need to do their own research beyond what is read about or discussed in class. Disciplines that involve learning to work with clients or with groups are well suited to collaborative learning techniques such as role-playing. Teaching, business, or social work scenarios where students need to practice the kinds of verbal interactions they will have as professionals can also serve as the basis for effective cooperative activities.

When asked about the advantages of collaboration, university students mention the following:

- seeing others' points of view;
- more enjoyable to work with others;
- solving problems in ways they have never before considered;
- "two heads are better than one."

Disadvantages of Collaboration

Possible disadvantages of collaboration are similar to those associated with student presentations and can include students diverging from main points you want them to focus on and developing misconceptions. Furthermore, some topics might not be amenable to cooperative learning and might better be suited to other techniques, such as a lecture on gravity for a physics class or a lecture on voltage, current, and resistance for an electrical engineering class.

Collaborative techniques can also have pitfalls from the student's perspective. For example, when asked about the downsides of collaboration, university students mention the following:

- some students dominate so that others cannot make their opinions heard;
- some students do all of the work while slackers do none;
- finding a mutually agreed-upon time to work together outside of class may be difficult;
- students not showing up for work sessions;
- disagreements arise among group members;
- time is wasted when activities go off-topic.

Evaluating Collaboration

Considering the questions or criteria we proposed earlier, we find that collaborative activities can rate very highly in motivation, as most students enjoy working together, especially during class sessions. They can also rate highly in addressing a wide range of students' backgrounds and interests, especially if expressions of different points of view are encouraged. Efficiency and effectiveness, as is the case with discussions, are clearly affected by instructors' expectations and how clearly these are expressed to students. Less of the instructor's preparation time can be required than for some methods like lecturing, but as is the case with discussions, students will generally benefit from more instructor input. Finally, cognitive level is to a great extent dependent on the purpose of the activity—activities used to review information might be moderate, and activities involved in conducting research, synthesizing material, or creating new works could be rated very highly.

Improving Collaboration

The following are suggestions for using cooperative teaching techniques:

1. Set up ways to monitor group work effectively throughout the process, not just at the end. This ensures that everyone contributes and that misconceptions about content do not develop.

2. Have each student provide a brief outline about his or her contribution and individual research area. This also helps you in assigning grades later.

3. Break down tasks into goals and subgoals, and set up due dates for smaller goals throughout the project or class session devoted to group work. This ensures that students stay on track.

4. Assign and vary roles. This enables shy students to report back to the class for groups and prevents groups from being dominated by single members. Roles might include reporter, recorder, leader, and monitor.

5. Keep in mind that the number of people you assign to groups affects the length of time the assignments take. For example, it takes a group of five longer to process each member's responses than a group of three.

Collaborative Techniques

In this section, we describe different types of collaborative learning techniques that you can employ. We also include suggestions for making them work.

1. Study partners or dyads: Having students review materials in pairs can be useful (Spurlin, Dansereau, Larson, & Brooks, 1984). Here are some guidelines: If one student is acting as a "recaller" to review material and the other is serving as an active listener, make sure students switch roles frequently. If students are reviewing material for a test, the recaller should do so without open notes/books in front of her or him. The listener or learner should be an active listener, responding with questions like "Can you tell me more?" or "Can you give me an example?" rather than simply uttering, "Uh-huh" or "Good."

Usually the recaller profits the most from the activity, although both students are apt to learn better than if they had studied alone (Lambiotte, Dansereau, O'Donnell, Young, Skaggs, Hall, & Rocklin, 1987; Lambiotte, Dansereau, O'Donnell, Young, Skaggs, Hall, & Rocklin, 1988).

2. Tutoring: Student-to-student tutoring can be effective in helping students who do not know the material as well and could benefit from in-class tutoring or outside tutoring, such as from an on-campus tutoring center. Tutoring, along with other types of student teaching, needs to be monitored to ensure accuracy and prevent misconceptions. Additionally, classes that involve tutoring should not involve it so much that students feel that they themselves are not learning. Finally, tutors can fall prey to several kinds of illusions about students' knowledge during tutoring sessions (Graesser, D'Mello, & Person, 2009), including that students possess more knowledge about a topic than they actually do, that students have learned more in a tutoring session than they actually have, and that students understand what tutors are saying and the feedback tutors provide.

3. Research projects: In conducting cooperative research projects, student groups can divide up work in clearly defined ways, with all students submitting outlines or plans of their research areas. Make sure that you can differentiate each student's contribution to a larger work. This allows each student to develop an area of expertise and prevents "slackers" from failing to contribute. It also prevents overly responsible students from overtaking and com-

pleting the work of others. And it helps the instructor adequately assess each person's contribution in making grading decisions.

4. Games: Variations of the *Jeopardy!* TV quiz show can put students in the highly motivating roles of creating and moderating quiz questions and serve as fun ways for class members to review terms. Other types of team games can enable students to enjoy friendly competition while reviewing materials for tests, perhaps as they compete for improvement scores from pre- to post-quizzes (Slavin, 2011a). Also, online games or online group competitions can be motivating for students.

5. Role-playing: In realistic scenarios such as teachers-in-training enacting parent-teacher conferences, social work students enacting interactions with clients, business consultants working with customers, and so on, role-playing works well. Role-playing can be highly motivating for students if situations are well defined, realistic, and somewhat controversial (e.g., role-playing parent-teacher conferences involving presenting a student's poor test scores).

6. Jigsaw (Aronson, 2000): In this variation, students are placed into home groups of a predetermined number that corresponds to the number of topics you want students to cover. We typically divide students into groups of four. This works well if material divides easily into four subtopics, such as four stages of a process.

Students in their home groups count off, numbers one through four. All of the number-one students have the same topic, maybe the first stage of enlightenment, an initial stage of grief, or Piaget's stages of cognitive development. Each person goes to an "expert group" with other students who have the same numbers and topics. They study their individual topics within the expert group and prepare to teach their topic to their home group.

Although this kind of activity can be highly motivating to students, the instructor must carefully monitor information that students teach to prevent misconceptions. Additionally, it can encourage students to focus only on their own topics that they will be expected to teach at the expense of others. A way to prevent these things from happening can include following up with a quiz (Aronson, 2000; Aronson, Blaney, Stephen, Sikes, & Snapp, 1978).

7. Structured controversy: This type of activity can work better than a debate because it ensures that all students participate, whereas larger debates can be dominated by a few individuals. It also encourages students to develop rational arguments in favor of or against positions that they might not be inclined to support—a valuable way to develop higher level thinking for students who might not deeply consider other perspectives on an issue (Johnson & Johnson, 1985; Johnson, Johnson, & Smith, 1996). Finally, rather than establishing a winner and a loser, as in a debate, the goal with structured controversy is for each group to develop its own consensus from group members' disparate views (Johnson & Johnson, 1985). This activity has been

used for various topics in college classrooms, such as biology (Khourey-Bowers, 2006).

With this type of activity, it's useful to divide your class into small, even-numbered groups and assign pro and con points of view through some random means or by counting off. The smaller subgroups of pros and cons meet separately to develop their arguments for a designated amount of time. A specific issue can serve as the topic for debate (e.g., the death penalty, genetically modified crops), or a controversial statement, such as "Over-the-counter genetics test kits are valuable tools for enabling consumers to 'take charge' of their own health care."

When preparations are complete, one subgroup (e.g., the pros) presents its arguments while the cons quietly listen. Following this, the opposing side presents its arguments while the others listen. An additional step might involve having students reverse roles and present the opposing point of view (Johnson, Johnson, & Smith, 1996). For the last part of the activity, each group attempts to resolve conflicting perspectives and arrive at a consensus.

In a variation of this activity that we have used, you can have all of the "pros" get together in a large group while all of the "cons" get together in a similarly large group to develop their arguments. With this, as with all debate-like activities, the amount of preparation and research that goes into students' arguments can largely determine the depth and ultimate success of the activity. If preparation time is brief, arguments are likely to be more superficial.

8. Problem-based learning (PBL): Since the 1990s, this approach has been adopted in many medical and dental schools as an alternative to traditional lecture-based forms of education (Feather & Fry, 2009). In this variation, students are divided into problem-solving groups and are presented with a problem, situation, or scenario that they need to solve. In the medical school example, a patient with a particular constellation of symptoms may be described. Students discuss the case, research the possible medical conditions, develop a diagnosis, and recommend a treatment plan.

As Feather and Fry (2009) explain, there are two major kinds of PBL: a "short case version" and a "progressive version." A short case involves the presentation of a brief case or scenario, such as the following:

> Blake is a thirty-three-year-old male residing in Hawai'i who has been in generally good health. Several weeks after returning from a vacation, he developed flu-like symptoms. He did not seek medical attention. After having the flu-like symptoms, he has developed numbness, headaches, forgetfulness, and a general lack of energy that has persisted for several weeks.

The second type is a progressive-release version in which part of the scenario is presented and discussed by students, then more information is given. In the above scenario depicting symptoms of Lyme disease, Blake's condition and symptoms might be described initially in more detail, withholding the information that his travels involved backpacking in Vermont (an area where ticks can carry Lyme disease) and his residence in Hawai'i (where ticks carrying Lyme disease are not found and the disease is therefore rare). Progressive information might also be presented regarding his results from various lab reports, discharge records, and so on.

Both kinds of PBL involve the use of facilitators for groups who encourage, provide feedback, assess, and guide students. Facilitators should be knowledgeable about content and trained in working with PBL.

As Feather and Fry (2009) explain, students who participate in PBL exhibit learning that is "less detailed . . . [but] more relevant, deeper and more lasting" (p. 429). Further, students enjoy working with veridical scenarios that resemble the kinds of problems that will face them.

INTERNSHIPS AND SERVICE LEARNING

Internships provide valuable occupational training for students in many disciplines. As an example, the need for internships in the experimental sciences is described by Hughes and Overton (2009): "Graduates have made it clear that they are generally ill-prepared for the practical issues they have to address in their early employment [Brown, et al., 2005] possibly because of reduced quantity and quality of practical work offered on courses" (p. 235).

The importance of internships for occupational preparation seems indisputable. Yet internships have raised a number of legal questions over the last several years, starting with a basic question: What is an internship? When should an intern actually be a paid employee? Thus, we include the following discussion of legal criteria for internships about which we believe professors and instructors should be knowledgeable.

The U.S. Department of Labor guidelines for determining whether a person is a trainee or should be a paid employee were released in 2010 (Lipka, 2010). To be considered an internship, six criteria must be met:

> The internship, even though it includes actual operation of the facilities of the employer, is similar to what would be given in an educational environment;
> The internship is for the benefit of the intern;
> The intern does not displace regular employees, but works under close supervision of existing staff;
> The employer that provides the training derives no immediate advantage from the activities of the intern, and on occasion its operations may actually be impeded;
> The intern is not necessarily entitled to a job at the conclusion of the internship; and

> The employer and the intern understand that the intern is not entitled to wages for the time spent in the internship. (U.S. Department of Labor Wage and Hour Division, 2010)

The release of these guidelines raised the ire of thirteen university presidents who, in April 2010, wrote to Hilda Solis, the U.S. Department of Labor secretary, requesting that student internships not be regulated. Ross Eisenbrey, vice president of the Economic Policy Institute, sent another letter to Solis that stated:

> What the law requires is, in one sense, very simple—that employers pay at least the minimum wage to employees whom they employ. This is as true for students as for other trainees, and has been the law for more than seventy years. When an internship is not employment, but is truly an educational experience for the benefit of the intern rather than for the economic benefit of the company, there is no requirement that the intern be paid. (Eisenbrey, 2010)

Thus, the purpose of an internship is to teach the intern. So, a summer job involving filing, arranging materials, hauling items, or answering the phone is not likely to be an educational experience for a student intern (although some aspects of answering calls might be!). Here, the benefit is for the employer, not the student. The student's activities might well take the place of hiring an additional employee—again, not to the student's benefit, but to the employer's. Appropriate internships are carefully monitored experiences that build students' knowledge and skills about medicine, engineering, business, teaching, and many other fields.

Advantages of Internships

Many professions require internships or service-learning experiences as crucial aspects of students' preparation (e.g., social work, education, business, medical professions, etc.). Internships are especially helpful for enabling students to (a) make career choices, (b) have work experience, (c) learn about social issues (e.g., homelessness, domestic violence), (d) create a sense of altruism/community involvement, (e) develop marketable skills and increase employability, and (f) facilitate communication and social skills in genuine contexts.

These features can also be considered the advantages of internships. From an instructor's perspective, the major advantage is providing realistic work-related or service-learning experiences in real-world contexts that cannot be duplicated in the classroom. Thus, students can apply seemingly abstract principles or theories that they are learning about in your classes to actual work-related scenarios.

Disadvantages of Internships

The disadvantages of internships for instructors can include spending additional time making contacts for placements, helping students find placements, monitoring their progress, and helping them resolve difficulties that might emerge. Since instructors are usually not present at placement sites, an additional difficulty is the instructor's lack of control and direct supervision over events.

Evaluating Internships

Generally, taking into account our previously proposed questions for evaluating instructional methods, we find that internships and service-learning experiences can rate highly in motivation and in addressing the range of students' backgrounds and interests, especially if students are involved in selecting their own internships. These experiences can vary in efficiency, effectiveness, and cognitive level depending upon clarity of internship guidelines, the extent to which instructors monitor and tie experiences to coursework, and goals for students' accomplishments during these experiences.

Improving Internships

Hughes and Overton (2009) argue that stages in the work/internship placement should include:

1. "Finding the placement" (p. 233): Does the instructor or college assist or do students find their own placements?
2. Defining the partnership: What are the responsibilities of the student, the company, the student supervisor? These matters should be set out in a handbook.
3. "Preparing the student" (p. 233): Students should understand resume-writing, interviewing, and workplace expectations.
4. "Maintaining contact with the student" (p. 234): Students and faculty should keep in touch throughout the placement, whether by e-mail, phone, or visits.
5. Assessment: Appraisal, in terms of a description of personal progress, should be tied to the workplace experience through such devices as an experience portfolio, report, or log.

To these stages, we add other criteria related to health, safety, and knowledge of particular legal issues that are foundational to certain disciplines, such as health care and engineering, among others. For example, Dickens and Arlett (2009) mention the importance of conforming to health and safety standards. Although their area of interest is engineering education, health and safety standards are of concern in all areas. As they mention, universities have legal responsibilities for students in job placements. Even in social science internships, making sure that students are in environments that are safe and well supervised is crucial.

Furthermore, basic legal knowledge and effective communication skills may also be foundational. For example, among the knowledge that Dickens and Arlett (2009) identify as important for engineers is that concerned with clear communication, entrepreneurship, intellectual property, ethics, and sustainability knowledge.

Finally, professional associations and institutions may have other and more specific guidelines that need to be followed when training people for internships, such as the provision of HIPAA training about patient privacy in medical contexts, APA training for students in psychological settings, FERPA training regarding family privacy for students in educational contexts, or privacy issues related to clientele and intellectual property in the business world.

You are encouraged to contact your professional association regarding discipline-specific guidelines, as well as your higher education institution and the institutions to which you are sending interns (schools, hospitals) to familiarize yourself and your students with guidelines and regulations. Finally, it is advisable to orient students to appropriate professional expectations for attire and behavior in the workplace.

WRITTEN ASSIGNMENTS

Written assignments ranging from informal written responses to formal research papers play a major role in secondary students' learning in most disciplines. In this section, we describe advantages and disadvantages in using written assignments and provide suggestions for improving students' learning through written assignments.

Advantages of Written Assignments

The advantages of assigning written work include (a) promoting students' critical thinking, (b) enhancing writing skills, (c) expanding interests, and (d) promoting discipline-specific professional writing skills.

Disadvantages of Written Assignments

Among disadvantages of writing tasks are (a) the time they consume for both students and instructors, (b) the ease with which students can simply download papers from the Internet and claim them as their own or use less-than-credible references from the Web, and (c) the failure to provide the best learning experience in performance-oriented fields, such as the arts, engineering, teaching, and social work.

Evaluating Written Assignments

Again, taking into consideration the questions we proposed earlier in the chapter, we find that written assignments can rate very highly on learning effectiveness and cognitive level of learning involved. They can rate less highly on students' motivation, especially if a great deal of work is involved, although students can become more highly motivated if they have selected their own topics or if they are especially interested in assigned topics. Written assignments can also rate lower than some other instructional methods on addressing students' varying backgrounds and abilities, as some students are less proficient in writing than others (however, for these less-proficient writers, such assignments and careful writing instruction might be exactly what is needed). Such assignments require a great deal of the instructor's time and effort unless, of course, you are fortunate enough to have a teaching assistant grade and respond to drafts.

Improving Written Assignments

We like the distinction between formal, high-stakes writing (research papers and the like) and informal, middle- to low-stakes writing (essays, journals, less formal response papers) where students apply theories and concepts to their own experiences (Elbow and Sorcinelli, 2011). High-stakes assignments, such as research papers, can serve as capstone projects for courses, while low-stakes writing can be used by students to work out ideas, connect with material, and develop fluency and practice with writing. We offer the following suggestions for structuring written assignments to help students learn most effectively.

1. For larger, high-stakes assignments (research papers, literature reviews), assign students to submit segments in progressive parts. For example, a set of references is due on one day, an outline is due the following week, and a completed first draft is to be submitted the third week. This approach requires students to work consistently on a paper during the course of several weeks, yields better writing, and minimizes the chances of night-before-the-paper-is-due plagiarism from the Web.
2. For all written assignments, make sure that your directions and prompts are clear and specific. Students should not have to second-guess what the instructor wants, especially in response to essay test items.
3. To dissuade students from citing sources from the Internet without considering the varied degrees of credibility that Web sites can contain, you

can require that they include only references from refereed journals or books and explain to students what refereeing means in your field.

> Just because someone can navigate to a Web site—or even knows how to construct Web sites—does not mean that the person can identify reliable, authoritative resources from the Web or know how to best interpret and communicate a Web site's content via a well-supported argument. In other words, technological competence alone does not equal information and communication technology (ICT) literacy. (ETS, 2005, p. 2)

Thus, we suggest that instructors offer students guidance that is specific to their subject area, using the following kinds of questions as starting points: What is a refereed source? What constitutes credibility on Web sites in your field? What are the vested interests of those posting this information? (Iding, Crosby, Auernheimer, & Klemm, 2009).

Improving Your Responses to Student Writing

Are instructor comments on student papers useful? If so, which kinds are most useful and in what kinds of instructional contexts will students use instructors' comments to improve writing? Furthermore, is peer writing response an effective tool for improving student writing? How might instructors optimally employ it?

First, Iding (1994) concluded that effective instructor comments should be *positive*—in the sense of encouraging—and *collaborative* rather than discouraging, *complete* and *meaningful* (not consisting of editorial abbreviations, like *awk* for awkward, that students do not understand) (Dohrer, 1991; Zellermayer, 1989), and clearly tied to *specific* examples in their writing (Ziv, 1984) so that they can see to what you are referring. Furthermore, the context in which you provide comments can affect their usefulness. Iding (1994, pp. 331–32) recommended the following, derived from the work of Applebee (1984), Dohrer (1991), and Hillocks (1982; 1986). These include:

1. Give students chances to revise. Students are less likely to apply comments made on one assignment to other, different assignments unless they are required to revise the current assignment based on your comments.

2. Relate your comments to issues you cover in your instruction. Perhaps you are focusing on how to write effective introductions or how to write a method section for an experimental research paper. Focus most of your commentary on those topics.

3. "Keep comments aligned with class goals" (Iding, 1994, p. 332). If you claim to value content more than mechanics in grading, but most of your comments are about mechanics, then you are sending a mixed message.

4. Be collaborative, not just evaluative. This can require a major shift in focus for some instructors. Try asking questions, pointing out where more

information is needed, requesting further explanation for what is unclear, while also mentioning aspects of the paper that were well done.

5. Consider comments students find useful. For example, Iding (1994) found that undergraduate students selected the following types of comments as most useful from their instructor: requests for additional information about a topic, comments about specific sentence structures, and comments about the overall structure of a paper. Iding and Greene (1995) discovered that students selected the following types of comments from their peers as most useful: requests for additional information, comments about mechanics, requests for clarification, praise, and comments about sentence structure and topic development.

Improving Students' Responses to Peers' Papers

Some instructors may not have the time to respond to drafts of student papers. In such instances and in situations where you wish to work further with improving student writing, you can assign classmates to respond to each other's drafts. However, these activities should be carefully structured to make them maximally useful. Through our extended use of peer responses and prior research, we derived the following recommendations for instructors (Iding & Greene, 1997; Iding & Greene, 1995; Iding, Greene, Fukunaga, & Ige, 1996):

1. Give an introduction to effective writing response. Tell students what you're looking for and model your responses to a sample student paper with the student's name omitted.

2. Incorporate peer response activities throughout the term. Students may be uncomfortable, at least at first, in responding to others' papers. In our work, we found a large increase in numbers of comments from the first peer response exercise to the second (Iding & Greene, 1995).

3. Require peer response. Also, require that students bring completed drafts on the day that the peer responses will be carried out; otherwise what students consider to be a draft can range from an outline or one or two paragraphs to a complete paper.

4. Allow students to discuss drafts with peer responders.

5. Determine which is more effective for your students—responding during class time or on-line outside of class.

6. If possible, have more than one person provide responses to a single paper. If something is unclear to a single reader, a student author might discount that feedback, but if it is unclear to more than one reviewer, a change is more likely to be made. Also, some students simply provide more valuable feedback than others.

7. Emphasize that authors are the owners of their papers. Thus, it is up to the author to decide whether peer comments are useful or not and how to best make changes.

8. Create a collaborative "experimental" environment around peer response activities. Ask students what kinds of comments they find most useful from peers. Elicit their input on how best to structure peer reactions and how to improve responses as you progress through several rounds with subsequent assignments.

9. Employ a working model of guidelines about what to look for in responding to colleagues' work or a rubric you may have developed to guide your discipline-specific writing instruction.

Dealing with and Preventing Plagiarism

We find that each year we have to deal with some aspect of academic dishonesty or plagiarism. The most common type involves inadequate paraphrases in which sentences or phrases are lifted from other sources and a few words are changed. These usually can be detected easily by carefully reading student writing, as different writing styles in a single paper may be clear.

Another problem is submitting the same paper twice for different classes without obtaining both instructors' approval (in some cases a student working on a larger piece might request to have part of the paper count for one class and another part count for another class, a procedure that would be considered acceptable at institutions with which we are familiar).

You might check your university's policies for dealing with plagiarism and include the policy on your syllabus. Your institution has guidelines for dealing with this issue. At many universities, minor instances of cheating or academic dishonesty are dealt with by professors directly in ways they deem appropriate (e.g., failure in an exam or no credit with resubmission required for a grade) and more serious instances—relating to high-stakes exams, theses, or dissertations—are brought forward for further inspection by the department chairperson, graduate dean, or dean of students.

We do not accept papers that have improper paraphrases or uncited work. If there are merely a few sentence-level violations in an undergraduate-level assignment, we return the paper to the student and usually allow for revision if the assignment is of a low-stakes variety. We offer several handouts about proper citation of work and appropriately paraphrasing that we often give to students and use in teaching mini-lessons to whole classes if we determine that there's a need or if students request this instruction.

If a student plagiarizes a larger, significant piece of text, a whole paper, or submits works written by another student, a failing grade for the assignment is given. If academic dishonesty is part of an ongoing pattern or is associated with a graduate student's performance, further disciplinary action (e.g., failure in the course, contacting the dean of students) might be required.

Furthermore, if plagiarism involves high-stakes writing, especially at the graduate level (e.g., thesis, dissertation, or written take-home examination), we would contact the student's advisor, department chairperson, or dean.

We recommend making a copy of the student's paper to keep with any instance of academic dishonesty. This might be required if further action is taken or if academic dishonesty is found to be a pattern for a particular student.

Students who are non-native speakers of English can have difficulties in doing research and academic writing and may not be familiar with conventions regarding paraphrasing or appropriately citing work. It is often desirable to ensure that these students have extra tutoring about these topics. They may profit from on-campus writing centers that offer tutors who read drafts of student work and assist students in writing comprehensible English prose. (Students with learning disabilities affecting reading and writing may benefit as well.) Looming deadlines and embarrassment about English proficiency can be factors that contribute to some students' academic dishonesty.

In our experience, the best preventative approaches involve working with a student's successive drafts throughout a term rather than only assigning a single high-stakes assignment due at the end of the semester, thereby conveying to students who are learning English that you are most interested in meaning and ideas expressed in papers, not in perfect writing. Being available to consult with students about their writing or providing resources to assist them with writing can help to prevent plagiarism.

Some students hire editors to help them with theses or major papers. We encourage you to discuss this with faculty in your program to determine whether this is acceptable, whether you wish to create guidelines regarding this for your courses, and whether you discuss those guidelines with students. Engaging editors or other graduate students that point out grammatical errors and clumsy phrasing might seem acceptable and helpful—in a thesis, for example—although some faculty members and programs may be opposed to this practice.

In working with editors and others to fine-tune writing, students and faculty need to remember that there is a fine line between editing and rewriting. We believe that writing, even with stylistic errors or English language deficiencies, should be the student's own. To help ensure this, we recommend that advisors review copies of initial drafts with editorial comments along with final drafts. We also recommend that you consider adopting guidelines such as those proposed by the Editors' Association of Canada (2012).

Finally, there are Web sites in which you can insert text and have it evaluated for plagiarism, such as Turnitin.com. Your university might subscribe to such a resource. In many instances, you can insert a sentence or key phrases of text into a search engine and easily find out if the student has copied from another source.

CONCLUSION

In this chapter, we have reviewed the more common instructional techniques found in institutions of higher learning. New instructors can be expected to develop their particular instructional methods by learning effective strategies from colleagues, receiving feedback from their students, attending teaching workshops offered on campus and at conferences, and reading higher education newsletters and articles about teaching. Experienced instructors should also do these same things, with the goal of continually growing as effective instructors.

Chapter Four

Learning Materials and Technologies

Twenty to thirty years ago, a professor's major decisions regarding materials involved choices between using textbooks or compiled readings. Instructional or multimedia decisions involved using chalkboards or whiteboards, slides presented via overhead projectors and filmstrips. Biology and other science courses involved the use of realia—actual preserved animals for dissection and examinations of authentic specimens.

Today's college instructors are faced with a myriad of instructional decisions regarding computer-based enhancements and technologies. In this chapter we describe some of the basic decisions instructors make as they plan courses—coursepacks and textbooks, simulations and presentation software, audience response systems (aka clickers). Since instructional and computer-based technologies are being developed and updated continually, we do not attempt to provide an exhaustive overview but leave the ultimate decision making and updating to readers, who as incipient content experts will be responsible for also keeping up-to-date with instructional innovations in their fields. For readers interested in developing online courses, we deal with that topic in chapter 7.

READINGS

For many instructors, the primary decision involves what readings to assign: textbooks, coursepacks, PDFs of readings. In this section, we describe some considerations that might factor into these determinations.

The level of students with respect to the content being taught is a primary consideration. For example, if the course is introductory and provides a broad overview of a field, it may be useful to use an introductory-level textbook. Advantages can include broad and up-to-date coverage along with many enhancements, such as CDs and textbook-related websites created by publishers. Disadvantages can include the high costs of textbooks (most are well over $100) and sequencing of topics (should the instructor see another order as more logical).

The high cost of textbooks has proven prohibitive for many college students. As David Zhou (2005) explained:

> Publishers routinely sell identical copies overseas for only a fraction of the U.S. price. Last year, my friend bought for $60 an "international edition" math book, the identical American twin of which sells for over $100 more. . . . For students from families that can comfortably afford college, these inflated prices are unfair and annoying. But for students from less privileged backgrounds who pinch and work to pay tuition (which, amazingly, has increased faster than textbooks), expensive books can be a major barrier to higher education. (para. 4–7)

In response, publishers have developed lower cost alternatives, such as plastic-wrapped unbound versions of textbooks and textbook rental programs wherein a student might have access for a particular term. However, should the text be one the instructor hopes students might keep as a reference book for later use and for studying for licensure and other exams, the rental process might be less than desirable.

Of course, e-books are replacing hard copies in most fields and clearly represent the wave of the future. E-books are generally less expensive, accessible on a multitude of devices, including one's phone, and thus more readily accessible and portable. As of this writing, some cautions with e-books are related to how they are viewed. If downloadable in PDF or similar versions, they can be quite easy to work with, especially if students have software capabilities to annotate them. If viewable only online via the publisher's website, their utility for students (and their instructors) is greatly reduced.

In addition to refereed materials published through respected academic presses, there are movements toward providing freely available textbooks licensed through various sorts of creative commons and other websites. Here authors place textbooks online and specify that they may be used freely by other instructors. Of course, the greatest advantage is reduced cost, an important consideration if an instructor is teaching in a developing region or to impoverished students, a consideration that prompted the first author to use such a text when teaching in a U.S. territory. However, one must carefully vet such materials: if the site does not employ conventional refereeing and editing processes, one might find inaccuracies in the text. In the previous example, she simply mentioned to students the areas in which she disagreed with textbook authors or found information outdated.

Ideally, multiple authors submit to a text and a highly respected book exists online and can be adopted for students. In fact, some institutions and authors are working to provide peer-reviewed, freely available e-textbooks. In conjunction with these, errata spaces are also provided where professors finding errors that were not uncovered during peer review can post corrections.

COURSEPACKS AND SELECTED READINGS

Many instructors prefer to enhance assigned textbooks with supplementary readings, or they provide compilations of readings instead of textbooks (or a group of PDFs or a list of links for students to download their resources). In the past, instructors placed such supplementary readings on reserve at university libraries, in accounts associated with individual classes. Although today such resources are still available for particular uses—out-of-print manuscripts, for example—more instructors choose to use online means for sharing resources with students. Before we discuss this aspect further, we describe some of the advantages and disadvantages of compiling readings.

For graduate courses and seminars, particularly those addressing a specific research interest, such as the professor's research area, compiled readings are usually ideal. The instructor determines a logical sequence of topics and selects readings (generally current research or seminal papers) addressing these topics for the assigned topics to be addressed each week. Some advantages of this approach include the currency of the work that ties well with graduate students' research interests as they develop theses and dissertations. Another advantage is that the professor can expand upon his or her own research interests, exploring areas about which he or she knows a great deal and adding new and related topics for further examination.

An alternative to this approach is adding some articles to required textbook readings to enhance the textbook or to add more current perspectives (assuming that most textbooks, as secondary sources, describe work that is already one to two years old). Instructors can preselect readings and mention them on the syllabus or add them as the course unfolds, keeping in mind that students are typically more positively disposed toward assignments that are removed, rather than added. Thus, if readings are added throughout the term, it is best not to add many or to make clear to the students at the beginning that a certain number of readings will be added.

A further alternative (most appropriate with advanced courses or graduate seminars) is to have students add some of the readings. This can work well if students are already well entrenched in their fields, if criteria for selection are established, and if the instructor vets the articles before they are forwarded to the other students. This also works well if the instructor has provided or worked with the class to provide a set of criteria for evaluating the research in the articles. Students can then discuss and evaluate the articles. For example: Does the theoretical framework provide an adequate basis for the research? Are there alternative explanations for the patterns of findings? Sometimes, the very questions reviewers are asked to address in determining whether manuscripts submitted for publication are acceptable can serve as useful bases for students to begin to discuss and evaluate current research and to learn the criteria by which their own work will be judged.

If an instructor selects readings, it is incumbent upon him or her to provide the overall thematic framework that ties the readings together. The instructor must also ensure that their method of providing readings does not violate copyright or fair use. As we mention elsewhere, because references are easily available online does not mean that they are not subject to copyright restrictions. Thus, if readings are reproduced as PDFs or links are sent to students, the instructor needs to ensure that the materials are not restricted or in violation of copyright laws. Most universities have knowledgeable librarians who can provide guidance. Further, university and college libraries have guidelines on their websites. If such information is difficult to find, Stanford University Library and other well-known universities provide useful resources.

UNIVERSITY LIBRARY RESOURCES

In addition to subscriptions to online journals, many university libraries provide access to academic and professional books online that students and faculty can find useful. Thus, they can "check out" and access books on their own individual bookshelves. Further, if books or other materials are not available in hard copy or online, universities have access to interlibrary loan systems enabling users to request hard copies (usually for a limited checkout period).

FILMS, VIDEOS, FLIPPED CLASSROOMS

Films and videos can be valuable additions to any course, particularly for depicting scientific processes, actual historic events, speeches, and so forth. The first author finds brief films particularly useful for showing classical experiments in psychology—ones that are written about in many introductory textbooks but that are much more memorable as films. Other resources, such as the popular TED talks, can be used to show current research and to generate discussion.

The flipped classroom is another approach utilizing videos that has recently gained popularity (Mangan, 2013). With this approach, students view prerecorded material (videos of their professors' lectures or other videos presenting instruction) online outside of the regular class meetings. In the example Mangan describes, a chemistry professor provides short (ten minutes or less) videos accompanied by online exercises and quizzes that students complete as they listen. Then, during the actual class meetings, the professor helps students solve problems of the sort that previously were considered homework. This approach is gaining popularity because students do not have to spend lengthy amounts of time being "stuck" on homework problems that they could solve with expert assistance, and professors can provide that assistance at the time students need it.

PRESENTATION SOFTWARE

Presentation software appears ubiquitous at the time of this writing. Instructors who plan to deliver a lecture via whiteboard or chalkboard might feel like dinosaurs. However, some students and their instructors are beginning to complain about the overuse of presentation software—and those readers inclined to be critical of its overuse might find some interesting consolation in Tufte's (2006) brief publication.

However, let's examine some suggestions based on the authors' experiences and on research-based guidelines that can help instructors to use presentation software effectively. Before creating a presentation utilizing presentation software, consider the following:

- Determine whether it's necessary. If a somewhat open-ended discussion with graduate students in a seminar is planned, is PowerPoint necessary?
- Have a backup plan (for when power goes out, technology fails, etc.). This could mean having a hard copy of lecture notes or handouts based on the PowerPoint presentation for students. This is strongly recommended for instances where the reader acts as guest speaker in someone else's class—their technology setup might differ or something might fail.

When designing presentation slides, consider the following to best enhance the comprehensibility and appeal of the slides:

- Consult with instructional design experts or visit websites that provide their suggestions, such as Fulford and Tanare's (2011) useful guidelines for presentations, upon which many of the recommendations that follow are based.
- Use a sans serif font in bold, very large print. Stand in the back of the classroom in which you plan to teach to see if all students can actually read the projected slideshow.

- Use dark print against a contrasting background to maximize legibility. Keep in mind that students with visual disabilities will appreciate not using light colors on light backgrounds.
- Fulford and Tanare (2011) recommend using only one main point per slide.
- Use brief phrases as bullet points or "talking points"—the briefer, the better. Three to five words are ideal. If whole sentences or long passages are used, the audience is likely to fall prey to "split attention" effects (Sweller & Chandler, 1994): reading the slide ahead of the speaker then losing track of what the speaker is saying. Even if neophyte lecturers do not feel confident about lecturing, brief phrases should trigger their memory. Furthermore, author notes can be added that are only visible to the presenter should they seem necessary.
- Avoid distracting, unrelated animations and graphics. They only lead students' attention astray or, worse yet, irritate the audience.
- On the other hand, Fulford and Tanare (2011) recommend that presenters might consider adding interesting transitions and animations that direct attention to relevant points on the slide. Don't forget that simple features like an arrow can effectively direct attention.
- Keep in mind the power and memorability of good graphics.
- Use photos and graphics that create connections with the audience (Fulford & Tanare, 2011). As sources, consider familiar subjects or those that tap into students' interests.

During the presentation, be mindful of the following:

- Set up the laptop so the presenter is facing the audience. The presenter should make sure he or she is not standing in front of the screen or projector, blocking students' views.
- If there is a long passage, pause and let the audience read it (Fulford & Tanare, 2011).
- Look up at the class frequently, remembering that the main interaction should be between the speaker and the class, not the speaker and the laptop (or the material). Pause and ask for questions, or build questions into the presentation beforehand.

BLACKBOARDS, WHITEBOARDS, AND INTERACTIVE WHITEBOARDS

During the past century, the blackboard has likely been the most popular form of "multimedia" used in the classroom. The blackboard and its newer variants—green boards and white marker boards—are still probably the most popular visual aids to appear in classrooms globally, when considering the predominance of poverty in many less-developed regions.

Here, too, one is cautioned to use contrasting colors that are easily visible, to write largely and clearly, and to minimize the amount of time facing the board with one's back to the class to maintain some level of interactivity with the students.

Make sure that the board does not have too much information on it, and be sure to erase incorrect information—wrong answers to worked-out problems and so forth—as visuals are highly memorable and students can mistakenly remember the incorrect information.

Improvements on the traditional blackboard or whiteboard include interactive whiteboards that connect a traditional whiteboard with an instructor's computer. Thus, an instructor can capture what is done on the board with their—and others'—computer screens and project what happens on the computer screen with the instructor's own whiteboard. This approach has appeal for those who are in different locations and need to collaborate on creative work, such as for an architectural drawing or storyboard or for simple problem solving as in mathematics. It also has appeal for those who intend to capture the day's board work so that students can refer to it later—a bonus for students with disabilities or other challenges with language processing or rapid note taking.

SIMULATIONS

De Jong (2011) provides a useful review of instruction involving computer simulations. As de Jong (2011) explains,

> Computer simulations are computer programs that have as their core a computational model of a system or a process. The system or process that is modeled normally has a natural world origin and the model that is created is usually a simulation (i.e., reduction and abstraction) of the real-world phenomenon (de Jong & van Joolingen, 2007). Simplification is used because: (1) it is hard if not impossible to fully model the real world; (2) a simplification often suffices for the goal for which the model is built and greater realism also has costs in time and effort; and (3) a simplification creates less cognitive load for the learner. (p. 446)

As de Jong describes, computer-based simulations have a long history of uses for training pilots and others in military contexts (e.g., for war games). However, simulations can be valuable instructional tools in many other areas, such as science and economics, where realia might be less accessible. For example, well-known simulations of virtual cadaver dissections can be valuable for students who need to learn about anatomy and physiology but who might not be inclined to go into fields like medicine where actual cadavers are necessary. Further, fields involving learning to diagnose and remedy problems, such as health care and electronics, lend themselves well to learning via simulations, until the point at which working with realia is necessary (de Jong, 2011).

Educational research involving the use of simulations indicates that they can be useful for students if enough supports are provided along the way, as well as suggestions for students to reflect upon the adequacies of their own understandings (or their metacognition) as they learn (de Jong, 2011). Thus, it's helpful for instructors to think through what they hope students will learn in the end: a progressively more complex representation of a scientific system; diagnostic and remediation capability in some domain; or application of some type of scientific principles (e.g., hypothesis generation and testing). Once an instructor determines what their learning goals are, optimal simulations can be selected to achieve those goals.

CLICKERS AND AUDIENCE (OR STUDENT) RESPONSE SYSTEMS

Clickers and audience or student response systems can be profitably employed, often in large lectures during which instructors want to make sure students understand before moving on to subsequent topics. The use of clickers also provides a good way of ensuring student participation and attention, particularly if students' performance is counted toward course credit. As Ravi Vatrapu, Professor of Human-Computer Interaction at Copenhagen Business School (personal communication, October 3, 2011) recommended, the use of clickers is also helpful for determining misconceptions and misunderstandings without embarrassing students. With these systems, the instructor determines questions asked or polled, and each student is equipped with a clicker enabling him or her to respond to these questions via Wi-Fi technology so that responses are captured and automatically tallied.

PROBLEMS WITH TECHNOLOGIES IN THE CLASSROOM

Finally, it is important to recognize that teaching via modern technologies is not free of problems (beyond, of course, those involving technologies failing at inopportune moments). For example, consider the following scenarios:

> While teaching a course on communications that was largely discussion oriented, an instructor noticed that several students brought laptops to class and spent much of the class immersed in their laptops. As he walked around the room, he noticed that at least two students were e-mailing and another one was looking at *Facebook*.

> A philosophy instructor noted that a few students appeared to be texting on cell phones during class.
>
> A biology professor who was teaching a large lecture class was annoyed by a cell phone ringing during class. To his surprise, the student answered the phone and engaged in a brief, although muted, conversation, despite irritated looks directed her way by other students.

In addition, instructors are concerned about students using other technologies, primarily cell phones for non-course-related purposes, during class. In an article in *Harvard Business Review* entitled "Multitasking 101" (2011) the authors described a study by Kraushaar and Novak (2010), from the University of Vermont, which revealed that 62 percent of the open applications on student laptops were unrelated to the class. Furthermore, the students who visited irrelevant sites earned lower grades than the other students. Instant messaging was found to be "especially virulent" (Multitasking 101, 2011, p. 34), a finding that likely would be no surprise to most readers.

One approach to coping with unwanted use of technology is for instructors to include statements in their course syllabi provided to students, such as the following, which works better in small classes than in large lecture halls.

> Professionalism involves basic courtesy, including no cell phones, texting, or non-course-related computer use during class. If you are taking notes on a laptop, please put the top down during class discussions out of basic professional courtesy.

Another approach to unwanted technologies in the classroom is to determine ways to embrace them. Ask students to find answers to questions during class discussions on their cell phones. Incorporate Facebook and Twitter into teaching. Enlist students' help and suggestions about technologies. Students can be surprisingly willing to help.

CONCLUSION

Our intention in this chapter is to draw attention to some of the major instructional materials and tools that instructors can use and to consider some of their advantages and disadvantages. Each reader's content, the level of their students, and proficiency with various kinds of tools, such as technology, determine which technologies instructors select to most effectively help students learn. As new instructors gain proficiency in teaching and experiment with newer technologies, they'll have a much wider range of choices upon which to draw.

Chapter Five

Assessing Students' Learning and Evaluating Instructors' Teaching

In this chapter we describe the process of selecting and creating assessments to evaluate students' learning and instructors' teaching efficacy. Assessing learning involves developing ways to measure whether students have achieved your instructional objectives. Results or data from these assessments are used to evaluate or judge against your set of course criteria whether students have learned and to what extent. These judgments can serve as bases for making decisions about assigning grades for classes or providing credit for academic-related experiences, such as completion of a culinary arts apprenticeship.

First, we elaborate on the purposes of assessment and introduce terms central to testing and assessment. Then we delineate the various common kinds of assessment or measurement items, their advantages and disadvantages, and ways to design effective items. We explain the process of grading. Finally, we describe the process of teacher evaluation and make recommendations regarding the construction of useful course evaluations.

PURPOSES OF ASSESSMENT

Clearly, assessments and related evaluative decisions can serve many purposes. At the most basic level, we can use assessments of learning (e.g., class presentations or performances, written assignments, portfolios of work, tests of various sorts) to evaluate whether someone has mastered a course of study, such as an introductory course in English composition or the fundamentals of conversational Japanese language. Thus a student can be determined to have met certain prerequisites in a course of study and be ready to move on.

Such purposes are patently obvious to anyone who has ever completed a course of study. But assessment data can serve other evaluative purposes. For example, assessment results can be used in evaluating whether a program has sufficient rigor to meet accreditation standards or whether students in a program are performing sufficiently well.

Assessment results can also be used to aid in evaluating

- whether students in professional degree programs (e.g., nursing, counseling, engineering, teaching) are ready for licensure;
- who can be accepted to or continue in a program of study;
- whose students are learning relevant content and whose are not;
- which students merit scholarships or other awards; and
- which programs at a university should be kept or cut.

As can be surmised from the above (and not exhaustive) list, the adoption and use of assessment instruments to collect data, the analysis and presentation of those data, and related evaluation decisions can be political in nature and used to serve various kinds of agendas, some less associated with improving learning than others.

However, the use of valid and reliable assessments to collect data should be central to your teaching, indicating what students are gaining or not gaining from your instruction. Furthermore, teaching evaluations can determine the ways in which your teaching is effective or ineffective and how you might improve.

TESTING AND ASSESSMENT BASICS

Prior to designing assessments for your classes, it's helpful to know some of the basic concepts related to testing. *Formative assessments* are used during instruction (a class, a quarter, a semester) to see where students are with their learning and how effectively teaching might be taking place. Often taking the form of quizzes or homework assignments, they can provide good indicators of what students understand so far and where they might be aided by further instruction.

The use of *summative assessments* takes place at the end of a unit or a term to find out what students have learned, usually for the purpose of assigning final grades and/or determining whether students have sufficiently mastered a particular course of content. The final exam is a prototypical example of a summative assessment.

Other terms that are central to evaluation and measurement include *validity* and *reliability*. *Validity* basically refers to a test measuring what it's supposed to; as in a test of conversational Spanish that is used to assess knowledge of topics that were covered in the course. This is referred to as *content validity*.

Another form of validity is *construct validity* (the construct is the characteristic being measured, such as shyness, intelligence, or musical aptitude). If a test has *construct validity*, the results should be clear indicators of the presence or absence of the characteristic being measured, and statistically the results should correlate with other measures of the same characteristic (*concurrent validity*). Another form of validity is *predictive validity*—in other words, is performance on a test related to subsequent performance in a target area? Questions about the effectiveness of SATs in predicting college performance or the relationship between GREs and graduate school performance are ones of *predictive validity*. Degree attainment and subsequent career success might be considered related to predictive validity.

Reliability refers to consistency of test results. In other words, if a student takes the same or another version of the same test (e.g., a standardized test that relies on an item bank), performance on the two should be similar. As is the case with validity, there are different forms of reliability, such as *test-retest reliability*, or the *alternate forms* we just described. Another type is *split-half* that refers to dividing items on a test in half and calculating a correlation between the two halves. If the result is a fairly high correlation, one could assume that there is a consistent measurement of the ability or trait being tested. Finally, another form of reliability involves *inter-rater reliability*, or a statistical estimation of how consistent two or more raters' ratings are, such as of essays or students' performances.

In the section that follows we examine several of the most common kinds of assessment items, their advantages and disadvantages, and provide recommendations for creating effective items of each type. Further, we examine item types in relationship to levels of Bloom's (1956) taxonomy, a process that Waugh and Gronlund (2013) use in their useful book on testing, *Assessment of Student Achievement*. This enables instructors to consider the cognitive levels being assessed and to help design assessments that mesh effectively and fairly with instructional goals. Anderson and Krathwohl's (2001) revised levels of Bloom's (1956) taxonomy, which were described in more detail in chapter 2, are as follows: remembering, understanding, applying, analyzing, evaluating, and creating.

As you examine these item types, consider your own assessment goals: the kinds of items or assessment tools that you select (or combination of assessment types) should match your instructional objectives or assessment goals. In simplest terms, writing goals should be assessed with written assessments, performance-related goals should be assessed via performances (although not all types of realistic performances are feasible), and so forth.

As Waugh and Gronlund (2013) explain, assessment methods can vary in realism, or the degree to which tasks "simulate performance in the real world" (p. 19). Creating a business plan, diagnosing an illness, or counseling a client would all be examples. Further, tasks can vary in their complexity, in the amount of time required for completion, and the extent to which "judgment in scoring" is required (Waugh & Gronlund, 2013, p. 20).

MULTIPLE-CHOICE QUESTIONS

Advantages of multiple-choice items include ease of grading and the possibility of covering a great deal of content in a short amount of time.

There are several potential disadvantages of using multiple-choice items as well. Generally, if considered in terms of Anderson and Krathwohl's (2001) revision of Bloom's (1956) taxonomy, most multiple-choice items measure recognition of correct factual information (i.e., remembering or knowledge level), although they can be designed to test higher levels. By recognition, students don't have to remember and recall the accurate response, they only need to pick out the accurate one from the set of distractors.

A further disadvantage from the instructor's perspective (and possibly an advantage for some students) is the ease of guessing. Grammatical and other clues in the item stem and other segments of the test can help one figure out the correct answer. Distractors that are longer or shorter than other options or apparently implausible can be eliminated. In general, if an item has four response options (three distractors and one correct answer) chances of guessing correctly are 25 percent (i.e., better than playing the slots at Vegas). An additional disadvantage is that a good multiple-choice test is difficult and time consuming to create.

Guidelines for Creating Multiple-Choice Items

Several authors, including Alexander (2006) and Waugh and Gronlund (2013), offer excellent guidelines for multiple-choice items. We summarize some of their points below.

"Design each item to measure an important learning outcome" (Waugh & Gronlund, 2013, p. 93). We (along with your students) recommend testing on important (not "nitpicky" as students might say) information that you really need students to know.

"Be sure that the problem is clearly and simply stated" (Alexander, 2006, p. 331). Thus, a lengthy and convoluted stem can easily create confusion before students even arrive at possible answer options. Your goal is to test

their content knowledge, not their ability to wade through excess verbiage. Alexander (2006, p. 331) provides the below illustration of a poor item.

> There are many issues that can be involved when teachers try to construct good multiple-choice questions. Among those issues some pertain specifically to the way in which the options are put together. Which of the following is most likely to be a problem in wording multiple-choice questions?
>
> a. There are too many choices.
> b. There are too few choices.
> c. The material was not taught.
> d. There are clues in the stem.

A better stem would simply be the last sentence of the above stem: "Which of the following is most likely to be a problem in wording multiple-choice questions?" (p. 331).

"Avoid unnecessary confounds" (Alexander, 2006, p. 332). As Alexander explains, negative words and alternatives like "all of the above," "none of the above," or "c and d" can also confuse students rather than testing for the content knowledge you're aiming to assess.

"Remove all extraneous clues in the stem or the options" (Alexander, 2006, p. 331). Grammatical clues and other types of clues in the item itself and elsewhere in the test can influence the effectiveness of your items. Most readers are likely to remember correctly guessing on a multiple-choice test, using clues in the test's items, and perhaps even performing well, despite being unprepared.

"Make sure that the distractors are sufficiently distracting" (Alexander, 2006, p. 332). Thus, distractors should be "plausible," as Alexander argues, and we would add that distractors should be clearly differentiable, as well. An example that would be considered poor in this regard is provided by Sternberg and Williams (2010, p. 520):

> Schizophrenic disorders affect approximately what percentage of the U.S population?
>
> a. 1%
> b. 1.5%
> c. 2%
> d. 3%

A better item that has more clearly differentiable distractors is provided by Sternberg and Williams (2010, p. 520):

> Schizophrenic disorders affect approximately what percentage of the U.S population?

a. 1%
b. 8%
c. 14%
d. 20%

Do not use giveaways or non-content-related material that you might assume all students would know, such as jokes, distractors, or "fillers." These can privilege native English speakers and presume cultural background that some students may not have.

For multiple choice (and all other item types) make sure that your instructions are clear to students. Should they circle, underline, or fill in the correct answer? Is only one option acceptable?

TRUE OR FALSE QUESTIONS

The advantages of true or false items are similar to those of multiple-choice items: ease of grading and wide content coverage. The disadvantages are also similar: a high guessing rate but, in this case, the probability of answering correctly by guessing is 50 percent. Another disadvantage is that the selection of a wrong answer or the selection of a "false" does not provide information about what the student actually knows about the topic (Waugh & Gronlund, 2013). Furthermore, true or false items are most often used to test knowledge level or remembering, in thinking of Bloom's (1956) taxonomy.

As Waugh and Gronlund (2013) suggest

> Despite the limitations of the true-false item, there are situations where it should be used. Whenever there are only two possible responses, the true-false item, or some adaptation of it, is likely to provide the most effective measure. Situations of this type include a simple "yes" or "no" response in classifying objects, determining whether a rule does or does not apply, distinguishing fact from opinion, and indicating whether arguments are relevant or irrelevant. (p. 111)

Guidelines for Creating True or False Items

- *"Include only one central idea per each statement"* (Waugh & Gronlund, 2013, p. 112). Sternberg and Williams (2010, p. 521) provide an example of a poor item, with many ideas, some true and some false:

  > There are 12 innings in a baseball game, 4 quarters in a football game, but only 2 periods in a basketball game.

- *Make your statements as clear and precise as possible* (Waugh & Gronlund, 2013).

- *"Avoid absolute words"* (Alexander, 2006, p. 334). These include words like "always" and "never."
- *"Word the statement so precisely that it can unequivocally be true or false"* (Waugh & Gronlund, 2013, p. 113). This can be difficult for instructors as students can, on occasion, quite effectively point out exceptions that instructors haven't considered.
- *"Statements of opinion should be attributed to some source unless used to distinguish fact from opinion"* (Waugh & Gronlund, 2013, p. 114).

FILL-IN-THE-BLANK, COMPLETION, AND SHORT ANSWERS

Advantages of fill-in-the-blank and short answers (also known as completion items) are that they can cover a broad range of material and can be relatively easy to create. They check for students' recall (not just recognition) of correct answers and are usually associated with the lower levels of Bloom's (1956) taxonomy: knowledge or remembering. Thus, they may be useful for determining whether students remember information or have read a particular text.

Disadvantages include difficulty in grading, particularly when students fill in answers that might be partly correct or indicate misinterpretations of the item.

Guidelines for Creating Fill-in-the-Blank, Completion, and Short-Answer Items

Sternberg and Williams (2010) offer useful suggestions, including

- *"Each question should have one main point and should contain only one blank—or several, in order, if responses constitute a list—for the student to complete.* More than one blank separated by portions of a sentence can cause confusion" (p. 521).
- *"All blanks should be the same length, thereby ensuring you do not give students clues about the relative lengths of correct answers"* (p. 521).
- *"The question should be specific about the form of the answer you seek,* without giving the answer away; this way, students will know what is expected of them" (p. 521).

Sternberg and Williams (2010, p. 523) provide an example of a poor item that can be answered in many ways:

__________ tells the musician to play loudly.

They provide a better alternative:

Forte indicates that a musical selection should be played __________.

ESSAYS

Essays (including full-length papers) are also frequently used to test students' knowledge. Advantages of using essays include their usefulness in testing higher level knowledge of the highest levels in Bloom's (1956) taxonomy. Other advantages include the latitude afforded students in creating answers. For those reading and grading essays, encountering different responses can be rewarding indeed. Furthermore, a good essay exam is much easier for the instructor to create than an effective multiple-choice test.

Disadvantages of essays include the time spent grading and the challenges of establishing consistency in grading criteria, particularly if different raters/graders are being used (the latter would be considered an issue of inter-rater reliability). If essay questions are not properly specified, answers can go in directions that the instructor doesn't intend or anticipate. Further, essays may not test a broad range of factual knowledge. Finally, due to what can be viewed as the "subjective" nature of essay evaluation, students might question the fairness with which their essays have been graded.

Guidelines for Creating Essay Questions

Suggestions for improving essay items include being precise about the kind of answer you're looking for: students should not have to spend a great deal of time trying to second-guess the instructor's intent. Examples of poor and good essay questions provided by Sternberg and Williams (2010, p. 525) are provided below.

> Poor: What is the general tone of the essays written by Huxley and Snow?
> Good: The essays of Huxley and Snow are both concerned with "the future of man." Do you find these writers generally optimistic or pessimistic? Point out the similarities and differences in their views, and present your views of the future of civilization in the context of these two writers.
>
> Poor: Describe the life course of a patient with Alzheimer's disease in terms of defining changes.
> Good: Identify the six stages of the phase model with respect to the life course of a patient with Alzheimer's disease. For at least three of the stages, give an example of a defining behavioral and/or physical change seen in a patient in that stage.

Waugh and Gronlund (2013) have useful suggestions for creating good essay items. One of the most basic is, "Formulate questions that present a clear task to be performed" (p. 135). As they argue, "Complex achievement is most apt to be called forth by such words as 'why,' 'describe,' 'explain,' 'compare,' 'relate,' 'contrast,' 'interpret,' 'analyze,' 'criticize,' and 'evaluate'" (p. 135).

There are typical suggestions for grading essays more reliably, as summarized by Waugh and Gronlund (2013). These include grading all essays in one session, grading without looking at students' names, reading and grading all answers to the same question before proceeding to the next, creating a "model" answer to compare to students' answers or a list of criteria for an "A" level or "B" level answer, and so on. If more than one person is grading, make sure that you agree on grading criteria and periodically check to make sure all raters or graders are consistent in the application of grading criteria.

You can grade holistically by assigning an overall grade to an essay or paper, or you can grade analytically by developing a rating scale or what is commonly known in educational circles as a rubric that contains a list of criteria with points associated with each one. An advantage to developing a rubric (particularly if it is distributed to students beforehand) is the increased clarity and guidance that is provided.

For example, in rating student research papers, you might include such criteria as (1) completeness of review of literature, (2) appropriate citation and precise description of research, (3) balanced examination of alternate theoretical frameworks or lines of research, (4) demonstration of clear understanding of the concepts and constructs being examined, (5) overall coherence of the paper, and (6) adherence to mechanical and grammatical conventions (e.g., MLA or APA style).

You could describe each criterion further to be more precise and attach points to each of the above criteria, creating an overall rating scale, indicating which criteria you value more highly. For example, criteria 1 through 5 in the above example might be worth 20 points each and criterion 6 could be worth 10. Within each criterion, you can designate point values to be assigned to particular determinations; for example, for a 20-point criterion, 0 is unacceptable, 10 is satisfactory, 20 is excellent or outstanding.

PERFORMANCES, PRESENTATIONS, AND PRODUCTS

Although performances and presentations can be considered examples of performance assessments, we discuss products here as well because there are many similarities in how such assignments might be created and evaluated.

Like essays, performances, presentations, and products share the advantages of tapping into the higher levels of Bloom's (1956) taxonomy, depending on how they are designed. Higher levels of creating would presumably be involved in the following kinds of assignments: creating conference-style posters describing original research and presenting them to the class; creating and performing an original modern dance routine incorporating locally appropriate indigenous styles; participating in a well-researched debate; designing and teaching a lesson to an elementary class; or developing a blueprint for an office building.

Disadvantages can include the time and effort spent by students in fulfilling these assignments. If clear guidelines are not specified in advance by instructors, varying degrees of levels of effort can be expected, with student performances and products ranging widely in quality. These kinds of assessments can be difficult to grade, particularly if students work in groups and if you have not carefully monitored their individual contributions.

Guidelines for Creating Performance, Presentation, and Products Assignments

You'll need to carefully specify all aspects of these kinds of assignments in advance and make your requirements clear to students. Waugh and Gronlund (2013) suggest doing this by first articulating your performance outcomes in precise terms, determining the context for the performance, the "degree of realism" (p. 150) required, and choosing the "method of observing, recording, and scoring" (p. 160).

Similar to evaluating essays, an instructor can score such performance assessments and products holistically or analytically. Holistic grading, as mentioned earlier, involves assigning a single overall grade. Analytical scoring (which we recommend for complex assessments such as these) can involve simple checklists for determining whether each product or performance has all the required parts or more thorough rubrics with points assigned to various criteria. For example, in the case of an oral presentation, a criterion in your rubric might be related to content, and another to some aspect of verbal fluency. In addition to the advantage of creating consistency in grading procedures, the presentation of rubrics or checklists to students before assignments are due provides them with a useful set of criteria that they can aim to meet. In our experiences, instructors' precision and clarity in providing these documents appear to ameliorate students' anxiety about such assignments.

FEEDBACK TO STUDENTS

In many cases you'll want to provide some kind of written (or oral) feedback to students along with their total score, grade, or completed rubric. (We discuss grading issues and procedures in the following sections and provide an extended description of feedback to written work in chapter 3.) Generally, your goals should be to provide feedback that is constructive and encouraging. Dialogic feedback that is much like the comments one would make in a conversation or an appointment with a student is recommended (R. Heck, personal communication, October 21, 2016), although sometimes appointments are needed. As Heck explained, "Not only are we 'assessing them' regarding course objectives, but we are also using such opportunities to guide their development."

GRADING ISSUES

The final act in evaluation of higher education courses, is of course, assigning grades—both for individual assignments and for the overall grade for a course. This process should be relatively easy if grading criteria are specified clearly and transparently in advance (as should be the case on your syllabus). Having such clear specifications, including statements about late policies, is a major way to prevent disagreements with individual students about grades. The following fictitious comments by students represent typical kinds of conflicts or questions about grades that arise, and that you should be prepared to handle:

"I had a family emergency. That's why I'm turning my paper/take-home midterm a week late. I hope you'll accept it." (The family emergency is unspecified.)
"Why did I get a B on this? I've clearly explained my answer and included everything you said you were looking for."
"I'm sorry I missed class last week. I didn't get the exam when you passed it out. Can I have a copy and turn it in next week?"
"I am turning this in late because my (printer/hard drive) crashed."
"How did you calculate my grade? I got an A on everything that I turned in and you gave me a B+!"
"How many points is this worth?"
"I got 20 points on the last assignment. The next one is also worth 20 points. Can I just skip it and still get a B in the class?"
"Can I write an extra paper for extra credit?"
"Can I revise this paper?"
"I know I missed class four times. But I turned in all of the assignments."
"I missed class and the quiz because I had the flu. Here is my doctor's note."

Most of these issues can be prevented or easily resolved if an instructor has statements about whether late assignments will be accepted, if penalties will be applied to late assignments, whether all major assignments must be submitted to earn a certain grade in the class, and whether attendance is required, and, if so, what constitutes an acceptable number of absences and what the penalty is for exceeding that number (e.g., a statement on your syllabus such as the following: "Attendance is required. Two or more absences [or whatever is acceptable at your institution] can result in a lower grade or failure in the course.").

Several of the remaining issues involve missed classes and late assignments due to illness, family emergency, and other reasons. These may involve instructors' judgment calls. In our experience, illnesses (particularly those accompanied by doctors' notes) merit accommodation, as would students' children's illnesses and other serious family emergencies. Many of the less serious excuses require your best determination, particularly with students with repeated—and often suspect—excuses.

Once you teach for a while, you'll undoubtedly accrue a compendium of students' excuses, many of them real and some rather amusing. For example, when the first author was teaching an online course, one of her students repeatedly submitted lengthy e-mails requesting extra time and explaining why assignments were late. Much to the instructor's amusement, the "excuse-making" e-mails were as long as the assigned papers.

Some of the issues mentioned above involve explaining grades or recalculating them if errors are suspected. Requests to explain grades are reasonable, so we take care to do so when students ask, even if we feel our grading criteria are already quite clear. As instructors, we are well aware of the possibility of errors and would make appropriate changes when necessary.

Other issues involve extra credit. For these, you need to establish your own criteria. It's best to do so in advance and to include them on the syllabus. In doing so, you avoid the appearance of unfairness that could arise if you are seen as making extra credit available for individual students when they request it.

Although we do not make extra credit available to students, in special circumstances (such as illnesses or emergencies), we do make an effort to allow students to make up assignments. In the case of an exam, we might create an equivalent assignment for a student to complete.

Here are other situations that may arise. We do not resolve them for you but provide suggestions for you to think about as you deliberate.

- A student from a background that could be considered to be disadvantaged has worked very hard and improved significantly in your course, but performance on exams and other products is not equivalent to that of other students. However, the student exceeds the page-length limit by about 25 percent on every assignment submitted. When you discuss this situation with a colleague, he or she contends that it's unfair to "lower" your grading standards for this student. Is there room in your grading system to consider improvement?
- An international student has difficulty with written expression. For this common scenario at today's universities, there are usually on-campus writing centers that will work with students' written expression. These

writing tutors are trained to help with expression only, not with providing content or writing students' papers for them. In our own experience, we take into account language background in grading, being cognizant of the challenges of writing a paper or completing a presentation in a second, third, or possibly even fourth language.

Other conflicts about grading can come up with other faculty members or within or between programs. Consider the following.

- "Nobody registers for his course. He's a hard grader."
- "He gives easy A's—profs like him are responsible for grade inflation."
- "It's easy to get an A in his class. It's communications (or education or some other discipline)."

Depending on departmental and disciplinary cultures at your institution, these could be concerns that merit further discussion, particularly if your class is the "outlier" with higher or lower grades than others in your field. It's likely that such an issue might not be a problem except when performance in your course is a prerequisite for other courses or admission to a program. New instructors or those who are planning new courses might examine the grading criteria of colleagues or have another colleague grade an exam to see if your criteria are similar.

GRADING PROCEDURES

Generally, many university instructors use percentage grading systems or points systems. In a points system, the instructor determines the number of points each assignment is worth, adds each student's total, and assigns grades based on predetermined cutoffs—or if one is interested in comparing students' performances to each other, one might employ a norm-referenced system, more commonly known as "grading on a curve." Thus, one would rank students and compare those rankings to the normal curve so that the central two-thirds would earn average grades or be within a standard deviation of the mean. This sort of process could be applied to individual assignments, such as particular exams, or to total numbers of points for the course.

As Sternberg and Williams (2010) point out, due to grade inflation, many students today consider a B to be "average" whereas a C previously was an "average" grade. So if you assign C's to the majority, the criteria might be considered "harsh." They also contend that other problems with such a grading system include implementing it in small classes or in classes where students are "generally excellent or generally poor" (p. 540).

With a percentage system, the instructor "scores each test or assignment on a zero-to-100 percent scale, representing a percentage of the knowledge a student has demonstrated" (Sternberg and Williams, 2010, p. 541). At the end of the course, the instructor averages the grades together and converts to a letter grade. As Sternberg and Williams point out, unless assignments are weighted, such a system could be considered unfair to students. If one test or assignment is longer or "worth more," it should be averaged into the final grade proportionally.

As we have reiterated, if your grading procedures are carefully specified on your syllabus, if they are transparent, and if assignments are returned in timely fashion, there should be few surprises for students. If some students have questions about grades, they should be easily satisfied by your clearly explained grading procedures.

TEACHING EVALUATIONS

A practice that has become ubiquitous in higher education since its origin in the 1920s has been students' evaluations of instructors (Calkins & Micari, 2010). Although this process emerged from the need for an "impartial and scientific means to gauge teaching performance, by the early 1960s student ratings had become a site of anxiety and often bitter contest between faculty and students and between faculty and administrators" (Calkins & Micari, 2010, p. 7), particularly where personnel decisions were affected.

Calkins and Micari (2010) describe questions of validity of evaluations and of student bias. As they explain, critics of the process suggest that instructors' gender, sexual orientation, and attractiveness may affect ratings. The use of evaluations in personnel decisions may counter their utility as instruments of instructional improvement.

Spoorem, Brocks, and Mortelmans (2013) explain that the utility of teaching evaluations is compounded by pressures to use the scores as metrics for institutional effectiveness. Furthermore, they point out: "the sometimes poorly designed questionnaires suggest that the architects of the questionnaire also lack common understanding or consensus regarding what constitutes good or effective teaching (Johnson, 2000; Knapper, 2001)" (Spoorem et al., 2013, pp. 599–600). They also do not display good psychometric properties, that is, reliability and validity. (For a list of good instruments, see Spoorem et al., 2013.)

Other researchers argue that many student evaluations of teachers "are simply derived from the opinion of expert teachers and do not necessarily measure important job components. Items generated by faculty, while valid and informative, may not capture aspects of teaching that are important from a student's perspective or that reflect student values" (Catano & Harvey,

2011, p. 702). In response, they used the technique of "critical incidents job analysis" with college students and "identified nine teaching effectiveness competencies: communication, availability, creativity, individual consideration, social awareness, feedback, professionalism, conscientiousness and problem solving" (Catano and Harvey, 2011, p. 701). They do acknowledge that their evaluation of teaching is not an evaluation of a course or its associated assignments. Nor, we add, is it an evaluation of student learning.

To add to the complexity regarding the validity of student course evaluations, Spoorem, Brocks, and Mortelmans (2013) explain,

> Student perceptions of learning might not always reflect actual learning (e.g., students could think they learned a lot during a course, even if they failed the examinations). And because student outcomes on objective tests are affected by other factors as well (e.g., prior knowledge, interest in the subject matter), they cannot be considered precise measures of actual student learning in a course. For this reason, a pretest is needed at the beginning of the course to estimate accurately how much learning individual students acquired at the end of the course. (p. 608)

We mention these issues to underscore the difficulty in gauging teaching effectiveness via written evaluations. (And if you'd like a humorous take on the topic, you might read about Naftulin, Ware, and Donnelly's classic Dr. Fox experiment conducted in 1973, in which physicians and psychologists rated highly a nonsense lecture delivered quite convincingly by an actor.) Also, if you wish to be more knowledgeable about the inception, rationale, and potential uses of teaching evaluations from the American Association of University Professors (AAUP), we recommend that you read its Statement on Teaching Evaluation (1975).

Rather than providing a contentious flashpoint between faculty members and administrators, we believe that systems of course evaluations should be designed to truly inform instructors and improve teaching—goals that can be more dynamic, constructive, and expeditious than simply making static judgments about teaching based upon a single course or initial teaching performance, limited student opinion, or colleague-generated rumors (either supportive or unsupportive, often having little to do with teaching performance and more to do with politics and competitiveness).

What's a new instructor or faculty member to do? Below we describe the typical procedures involved in teaching evaluations, ones that we presume you should be quite familiar with from the student side. Then we make suggestions for administering, interpreting, and enhancing the results of your evaluations with accompanying materials that demonstrate your effectiveness.

Generally, departments develop evaluation forms that instructors are obliged to adopt. These usually contain about fifteen to twenty questions about such issues as clarity, preparedness for class, fairness, and the like, with Likert scale response options (e.g., on a scale of 1, indicating that you strongly disagree, to 5, indicating that you strongly agree). There is also room for student comments.

On the last day of the course, the instructor leaves the room and someone else—a student or another instructor—passes out evaluations and provides any instructions if needed. Then the evaluations are collected in an envelope and delivered to an administrative office where the data are compiled and summarized by a staff member or retained until after the course is completed. Instructors are not allowed to see the results until after they submit grades, on the belief that seeing the results could create bias and influence the grading process.

In conjunction with this process, we have several recommendations for new instructors:

If your department does not have an evaluation form or does not require teaching evaluations (perhaps for teaching assistants or part-time instructors), make sure that your course is evaluated. Asking your department chair or dean for a recommended evaluation form could be a helpful initial step.

Should you be in a position to develop or adopt your own form, we recommend that you use one of the forms suggested by Spoorem, Brocks, and Mortelmans (2013). Use the procedures described above, making sure that a staff member or colleague retains the forms until after the term is over and grades submitted. If you need to have the data summarized, it's best to have a staff person or someone else do the inputting and summarizing.

Retain the evaluations and summaries, as these can be part of your teaching dossier. Documentation of teaching effectiveness (or nascent excellence) can be used for later job interviews or promotions. Even if the evaluation scores aren't as high as you would like, you can demonstrate improvement in subsequent terms. Remember, growth as a teacher is a good thing.

If you have latitude regarding which items are to be included in your course evaluation, leave out ones that don't apply well to your teaching or are unrelated or outside your control (such as items about facilities or technologies that are not applicable). If you leave them in, they may detract from your overall means.

If you have a choice about administering your evaluations online or in class, consider some of the benefits and drawbacks. In-class, paper-and-pencil evaluations have the captive-audience advantage of high response rates but the disadvantage of having someone input data and calculate results.

Online evaluations are the direction many universities are taking. The disadvantage with these is that if students are expected to complete evaluations in their spare time, the response rate is likely to be low, although those who do respond might provide more commentary than they would on paper-

and-pencil evaluations. A solution is to provide time in class for students to fill out their online evaluations—when you are not present, of course.

Accompany teaching evaluations with other means of demonstrating good teaching and improvement in teaching, such as by inviting other faculty members to observe your teaching and write summaries. Retired faculty members are often good resources for such tasks. Have more than one visitor per year.

Demonstrate other innovations in teaching, such as using innovative strategies or developing new courses. Add these to your curriculum vitae (CV) and be sure to mention such innovations in any teaching dossiers or summaries of your teaching accomplishments.

Make use of Centers for Teaching Excellence and other such units. Trained observers will visit your class and provide feedback and suggestions. Midsemester reviews may be offered by such units, enabling you to use their feedback and make improvements during the rest of the term. Such units may also offer videotaping services—videotaping you, scheduling a meeting with a trained consultant with whom to view the tape, and suggesting teaching improvements if necessary.

Viewing your teaching video is particularly helpful for providing a student-like perspective from which to self-evaluate and to better understand comments from teaching evaluations. For example, a naturally shy individual might find ways to more clearly infuse her enthusiasm for her content into her classes. Although most people don't like to view themselves on video, the experience also helps to reinforce the positive things you're already doing well.

In interpreting teaching evaluations, look for themes instead of allowing yourself to puzzle over the single comment that represents the outlier. It's best to pick one or two areas to work on and allow yourself to feel congratulated about the things you're doing well. Every instructor that we know has received some negative comments, so don't be discouraged by the one person who has an emotionally charged, negative response to you, to some aspect of the course (e.g., that it's required!), or to your appearance.

In documenting or summarizing teaching evaluations for promotion or tenure, we recommend that you focus on what you're doing well and how you've improved from when you started. Remember, most new instructors improve over time, especially if they actively work at it, try new methods, and make changes. Most wise department chairs and hiring committees recognize this as well.

Remember, if you're intelligent and diligent enough to pursue an advanced degree and to be hired for a university teaching position, you also probably have what it takes to learn to become a good teacher, capitalizing upon your strengths and building weaker areas into stronger ones.

Teaching, like any skill, and human interaction itself, is synonymous with learning and continuous growth.

CONCLUSION

In this chapter we provided an overview of basic concepts related to assessment with which higher education instructors should be familiar and should find useful. We described the advantages and disadvantages of various types of assessment items used to evaluate student learning and shared suggestions for creating effective items. Finally, we explained the process of teaching evaluation, its origins, and related controversies, and provided recommendations for creating effective teaching evaluation experiences that can inform and help to improve your teaching.

Chapter Six

Characteristics of Your Students

Who is the typical college student? According to the National Center for Education Statistics (2016), today's typical college student is female and white. More than 30 percent work full time, 38 percent are older than age twenty-five, and just more than half are pursuing sub-bacalaureate credentials, such as associate of arts degrees or certificates (Hess, 2011). In any event, the typical college student today is similar to what was once known as a "nontraditional student." In those olden days of the early and mid-twentieth century, the majority of students were nonworking white males who attended college full time.

Despite social scientists' best efforts at capturing typicality, when you become a college instructor, you recognize that college students as individuals have only one thing in common—they are enrolled in higher education courses of some kind. Individually, they differ from each other in a variety of ways, some of which influence how they learn.

The purpose of this chapter is to examine (a) thirteen characteristics of students that may affect how they learn or experience higher education; (b) implications and suggestions for effectively teaching and working with students; and (c) related topics such as motivation, stereotype threat, imposter phenomenon, and microaggressions. The thirteen influential traits are intellectual development level, identity development level, age, intellectual abilities, ethnicity/culture, race, sexual orientation, gender, disability, emotional and mental challenges, military service, veteran status, and motivation.

LEVEL OF INTELLECTUAL DEVELOPMENT

Although your students may range from under age thirteen (if enrolled in high school advanced placement courses) through their retirement years, it is possible for them to share some developmental characteristics, particularly with respect to their epistemological beliefs, in the sense of what they believe to be true about the nature of knowledge. Perhaps the best-known conceptualization of epistemological development in college students was captured by Perry (1970; 1981). He described three positions that typify how students progress in their beliefs about knowledge and what it means to know something.

Position 1: Dualism

The world is constructed of right and wrong ways of seeing things, and professors' roles are to tell students what those right answers are (and what will be on the next classroom test, of course). For instance, a professor was teaching a Linguistics for Teachers course, and one of the course activities was a debate about different methods of teaching grammar in elementary schools. Months later, she encountered one of the students who mentioned the debate and asked her what her real position was, on the apparent assumption that in class she had identified more that one position but had failed to identify the one that was "right" or "true."

Position 2: Multiplism

During this position of intellectual development, students recognize many different points of view or opinions and then consider all of the alternative perspectives are equally valid. In effect, students appear open to many points of view but are unable to distinguish how certain views may be better supported by evidence or logic than others. An example would be considering all opinions expressed in a discussion about a literary work as being valid but not being able to select which perspectives seem better reasoned than others.

Position 3: Relativism

At this point, different perspectives are evaluated and weighed against each other. Students develop the capacity to reason out the better point of view based on selected criteria or in contrast to some theoretical constructs—and even develop commitments to particular points of view. Demonstrating relativism, a student may challenge a professor or others regarding their points of view.

As an instructor, you should find it useful to identify learners who are reasoning dualistically and therefore could be considered to be operating at position 1. They seem obsessed with finding the "right" answer, even when your goal is to teach them thinking, reasoning, and research skills for use at higher levels, when there may be no single memorized right answer.

Also, you might remember that epistemological beliefs about the nature of knowledge and knowing in various disciplines have been shaped by textbooks, testing techniques, and prior teaching. So for some students, knowing about the human eye may involve memorizing anatomical terms, whereas for another student it can mean truly understanding the physiological processes that underlie vision.

As another illustration, in a Poetry and Drama class, a new instructor found out that students were predisposed to dislike poetry because they regarded the study of poetry as involving reading a poem, being told what it is about by their instructor, and then regurgitating the instructor's interpretation on an exam. So although they were pleased to learn that the approach in this new course would involve developing their own interpretations of poetry, they found this experience required some adjustment. This adjustment could be viewed as promoting students' movement beyond position 1 dualistic reasoning.

Clearly, epistemological beliefs are one aspect of development that may affect college learning, but there are other aspects of development, such as social development, which, as you can easily guess, can have a major impact on students' ability to learn or on their ability to derive a useful academic experience from going to college.

Here are suggestions for fostering relativistic or higher level reasoning:

- Create discussion and debate opportunities where students develop and support positions for arguments. Learning to develop arguments for positions that they would not necessarily select to support for themselves is one way to encourage their development of well-reasoned positions. Have students develop criteria for evaluation and, using these criteria, determine which arguments are most effectively reasoned.
- Develop written assignments that encourage students to provide strong support for their arguments. In the social sciences, support might consist of references to previous research. In literature or language classes, support might consist of quotations from a work of literature or from a literary interpretation.

LEVEL OF IDENTITY DEVELOPMENT

As we mentioned earlier, many of today's students fit the "nontraditional" category that was used in the past. They are older, may be married, raising children, and working full-time. Some are pursuing second or even third careers, and some might be retired and taking college classes as a hobby. As a result, it would be difficult to conceptually place all college students into a single developmental stage.

However, since many students still fit into the "traditional" adolescent and early adulthood categories, we find it profitable to consider other aspects of development that are crucial at this point. Chickering and Reisser (1993) conceptualized a theory of identity development that points out the multiple aspects of development that are taking place at this time:

- Competence in interpersonal, intellectual, and physical realms.
- Healthy balance of independence (free from being overly needy) and recognition of interdependence in terms of membership in a larger society.
- Emotional management in terms of expressing emotions appropriately.
- Identity development in terms of social and sexual aspects.
- Healthy interpersonal relationships and intimacy.
- Purpose in terms of vocation or life path.
- Integrity in one's values.

Although we do not believe it is necessary to belabor specific aspects of development in each of the above areas, we do think it is helpful to consider some of the major developmental challenges that face students at this stage. Moving away from home, adjusting to dorm life, experimenting with alcohol, and sexual activity can affect your students far more than that mathematics formula you're trying to teach.

Additionally, even older returning students may be working on aspects of determining their life purpose or adjusting to changed family situations, such as divorces or empty nests. In addition to your providing subject matter expertise, you may be a role model and serve as a person your students may consult for career and other sorts of advice.

C. P. Brus (2006) describes her own experience returning to college:

> Deciding to go back to school for a graduate degree after being in the workforce for many years is a daunting prospect. . . . I remember sitting in my unfinished basement taking practice tests for the Graduate Record Exam (GRE), trying to concentrate while half-listening to my two young daughters playing above me. I knew I would never get in, especially after the GRE math refresher course was canceled. It had been twenty years since I had taken a math course. But the terror of taking the GRE was nothing compared to the terror I felt when I received my acceptance letter. I knew I was smart, very smart, but I was also very rusty, unused to using my brain in traditional academic ways. I was also keenly aware that not only was I old enough to be some of the other students' mothers, I was a mother myself, with two young children, a neurotic dog, two aging parents, three jobs, a mortgage, and a marriage that was disintegrating. Was I nuts going back to school? Maybe, but I was in good company. (p. 31)

The following are suggestions for fostering students' identity development:

- Be available to discuss career options with students who are interested in pursuing further study in your field.
- If appropriate, mention career options in your field. Addressing questions like "What can someone do with a degree in chemistry?" (or philosophy or another field) can be helpful for students.
- Announce career fairs, clubs, volunteer, or internship opportunities for students interested in more involvement in your discipline.
- Be aware of offerings that your college's counseling and career placement services might provide.
- Recognize that students sometimes may need emotional support beyond what you, who are not a trained counselor, can provide. Refer students to counseling or other appropriate services when psychological support is needed. (More about this will be discussed later in the chapter.)

AGE-RELATED COGNITIVE DIFFERENCES

In addition to developmental differences, there are age-related cognitive differences between students. Your youngest students may be still experiencing brain development (Sowell, Thompson, Holmes, Jernigan & Toga, 1999), while your oldest students might be dealing with aspects of cognitive decline (Fabiani, 2012). First, from a physiological standpoint, brain development continues into young adulthood, particularly with respect to frontal lobe development associated with executive functions (Toga, Thompson, & Sowell, 2006) such as cognitive control, decision making, and risk taking. Further, the ability to interpret others' emotional states is associated with the late teen years and frontal development (Herba & Phillips, 2004; Yurgelun-Todd, 2007).

What does this mean for your students? Impulsivity and risk-taking behaviors are features of late adolescence and can play themselves out in your classroom as well as in the out-of-the-classroom lives of your younger students.

Furthermore, in conjunction with maturation of frontal lobes, younger students perform more quickly at tasks requiring speed or quick reaction times (Fabiani, 2012). In other words, information that is recalled or recognized might be done so much more quickly among your younger students.

As adults grow older, reaction times become slower (Fabiani, 2012). Middle-aged and elderly adults may experience difficulties in recalling information like names (Crook & West, 1990). What students studied in world history or introductory language courses as undergraduates might have been more than twenty years ago, rather than last year.

In addition to slower reaction times, the very elderly might experience working memory limitations (Fabiani, 2012), which include increased distractibility (Fabiani, 2012; Rabbitt, 1965). Depending upon a range of lifestyles factors including general health, education level, and continued mental stimulation, one's cognitive skills at an older age can be affected (Czernochowski, Fabiani, & Friedman, 2008; Fabiani, 2012).

Older students might also feel intimidated by younger students and out of practice with the educational enterprise, as the earlier quotation in this chapter from Brus (2006) clearly indicates. However, older students often have more realistic perspectives that come with increased experience in the world, extensive careers, and a range of interactions with a variety of people. They may be less idealistic and more able to see many aspects of a complex problem that might not occur to their younger counterparts. Furthermore, they might be more clearly intrinsically motivated to perform well, since they are voluntarily taking your course (and typically paying their own tuition!), rather than succumbing to parental or peer pressure.

What suggestions do we have for facilitating learning of students of different ages in your classes?

- Tests and activities requiring fast reaction times might be more difficult for older students, whereas activities that require thoughtful application of problem-solving skills for larger-scale problems might showcase older students' capabilities. Therefore, you might capitalize on the strengths of older and younger students by including activities and testing situations that do not completely advantage one group over another.
- In discussions, show by your respectful acknowledgment of all student contributions that you value younger students' as well as elders' points of view. Do not call on members of one group to the exclusion of others.
- Add suggestions for how to best study material and model problem-solving strategies that are useful in your discipline. This helps younger students learning how to study as well as older ones who might need refreshers.

INTELLECTUAL ABILITY

Historically, intellectual ability was conceptualized as a unitary entity labeled *intelligence*. Early on, this referred to a performance on IQ tests that categorized test takers as average (90–109), above average and superior (110-130), genius (130+), or below average (70–89) and mentally retarded (below 70). This notion of intelligence as a single unitary concept was replaced by later portrayals of intelligence that encompassed many different abilities (e.g., Thurstone's [1938] depiction of seven major mental abilities—word fluency, verbal comprehension, spatial ability, number facility, perceptual speed, associative memory, and spelling). A more ambitious approach was taken by J. P. Guilford (1967), who initially proposed that human intelligence was composed of 120, and later on, 150 abilities.

A popular current conceptualization was developed by Howard Gardner (1983; 1999), who argued that intelligence has seven areas: interpersonal, intrapersonal (within one's self), bodily-kinesthetic, musical, logical-mathematical, spatial, and linguistic. He acknowledges that others may exist, such as naturalistic and existential.

Another current multifactor conceptualization is Robert Sternberg's (2006) triarchic theory of intelligence, which encompasses analytic (skills similar to those required on traditional intelligence tests), practical (applying solutions to problems in realistic contexts), and creative (inventive) intelligence. This approach has been used as the basis for developing a test that has shown promise in predicting college GPA and is suggested for use in college admissions along with the SAT (Sternberg, 2006).

For instructors, it's useful to think of intelligence as a set of abilities or potentials a la Gardner's (1983; 1999) multiple intelligences or Sternberg's (2006) triarchic theory. Seen from this perspective, each of your students has strengths or potential strengths as well as weaker areas. If you view intelligence as a multifaceted set of abilities, you are less likely to view it as immutable or unaffected by instruction.

CULTURAL OR ETHNIC DIFFERENCES

Among other sources of differences are ones based on culture or ethnicity. For example, some researchers have investigated differences at work in how people of different cultural backgrounds process information, such as whether they are field dependent or field independent (e.g., Engelbrecht & Natzel, 1997; Kagan, 1974). The construct involves situating a visual stimulus in a context in which the person either shows that he or she is dependent on the surrounding visual background (hence field dependent) or not dependent (field independent) (Witkin, Moore, Goodenough, & Cox, 1977).

Instead of looking for performance differences among students and relating them to cultural differences, we find it more useful to be knowledgeable about possible dimensions upon which cultures may differ so that we can better understand our students' interactive styles, expectations about higher education, and performance in our classes. We find G. Hofstede's (1991; 2001) dimensions to be a useful starting point; however, before we describe them, we acknowledge the point that his son, Gert F. Hofstede (2009), raises about work that investigates cultural dimensions:

> One of the big misunderstandings of these dimensional models is that they describe each and every individual from a particular society and a related fear that this constitutes a pejorative value statement—in other words, a stereo-

> type. . . . Instead dimensional models describe the unwritten rules of society. That is, they describe expectations and norms about how to behave in social life, e.g., between parent and child, among members of different in-groups, different hierarchical levels, different ages and genders. Dimensional models by no means preclude the idea of variety and change in society; of course every society is immensely complex, with vast difference between its members and with change occurring all the time. (p. 16)

In addition to not reifying cultural stereotypes, we do not wish to promote cultural comparisons that imply cultural deficit models—the idea that students from non-majority cultures are somehow less than others (Suinn, 2011). We also acknowledge the burden on some students who might feel obligated to disprove cultural deficit perspectives in contexts where they believe that instructors and others may subscribe to deficit perspectives.

Hofstede's (1991; 2001; 2011) six dimensions upon which cultures may differ are as follows.

1. Power Distance

This deals with equality and inequality among people in a society. In societies with small power distance, people interact as equals in schools, at work, and with the elderly. In large power distance cultures, there are clear hierarchical distinctions in those same areas. According to Hofstede (2011) "Power distance index scores . . . tend to be higher for East European, Latin, Asian and African countries and lower for Germanic and English-speaking Western countries" (p. 10).

2. Uncertainty Avoidance

This relates to tolerance for and intolerance of ambiguity. In weak uncertainty avoidance situations, stress is low. People tolerate situations where change is possible and situations and persons are unpredictable. In strong uncertainty avoidance societies, higher levels of stress are associated with strong needs for structure. Authorities like teachers are seen as all knowing. According to Hofstede (2011), countries high in uncertainty avoidance include Latin countries, Eastern and central Europe, Japan, and Germanic countries; countries that are lower include "English speaking, Nordic and Chinese" (p. 11).

3. Individualism versus Collectivism

Whether members of the society see themselves as primarily members of groups or as individuals makes differences in how they act. Hofstede (2011) notes that countries that are more individualistic tend to be Western and developed.

4. Masculinity versus Femininity

According to this dimension, masculine societies are associated with competitiveness and assertiveness, and feminine ones are associated with modesty and caring aspects of life. According to Hofstede (2011), "masculinity is high in Japan, in German-speaking countries, and in some Latin countries like Italy and Mexico; it is moderately high in English-speaking Western countries; it is low in Nordic countries and in the Netherlands" (p. 13).

5. Long-Term versus Short-Term Orientation

This variable focuses on how much people are present oriented versus future oriented. Countries that exhibit short-term orientations include the United States, African and Muslim countries, Australia, and Latin America. Long-term orientations are associated with northern and southern European countries along with South Asia. Hofstede (2011) observed that students attributed their failings and accomplishments to luck in short-term societies, whereas students in long-term-oriented societies attribute these to effort.

6. Indulgent versus Restraint

This dimension refers to whether the society enables easy fulfillment of people's desires to enjoy themselves in various ways or restricts these desires. Indulgent societies are associated with North and South America, some of sub-Saharan Africa, and Western Europe, whereas restraint is associated with Asia, Muslim countries, and Eastern Europe (Hofstede, 2011).

You may recognize that dimensions such as these can be especially helpful in understanding student differences. Hofstede acknowledges that other dimensions may be valid as well. In this book, we concur and describe below specific kinds of culturally related differences that you might experience in teaching, several of which may be related to the Hofstede dimensions (1991; 2001; 2011).

For example, it can be profitable to consider whether your students come from collectivistic or individualistic societies. In individualistic cultures, individual achievement and competitiveness are highly valued in education systems. In contrast, collectivist societies value the welfare of the group, family, or village above the achievement of a single individual or their academic progress.

Many societies in the Pacific Islands, Asian countries, and Latin American countries share collectivist values. In these scenarios, the welfare of the group is most important. For these students, group achievement in cooperative activities or collaborative efforts work well.

It is also helpful to remember that students from collectivist societies might find it extremely difficult to balance the demands of higher education with family and other cultural demands, which might be high. For example, a college student from the Republic of Palau (in the Pacific) mentioned how her family viewed her educational aspirations as selfish, since they drew her away from her expected roles as mother and family member. Her familial and cultural roles and obligations were quite extensive and included financial obligations to family members in Palau.

Furthermore, collectivism and high power distance may be also related to the familiar concept of "saving face" in certain contexts. For example, a student might not want to show that he or she knows an answer to a question that the professor has posed if it could make another student who could not answer the question correctly look bad or if the answer contradicts with the professor's perspective or could be seen as critical of authority (i.e., the professor).

Cultural dimensions like power distance might also be reflected in classroom dynamics in other ways. In Samoa, a cultural leader or elder might act as spokesperson for a class or group and be deferred to by the group although that person might not be the most academically inclined. Understanding such dynamics and working with them will help your teaching to go smoothly.

In addition, knowing about culturally appropriate interaction styles can facilitate interactions with students and save you the potential frustration of assuming students are not interested in your class or not participating in ways that match your expectations. It is also important to consider student behavior in relationship to your own behavior. A well-known cultural difference can involve eye contact (e.g., Suinn, 2011). For example, students from Navajo or Micronesian cultures might not directly look at instructors; looking downward is considered polite listening behavior.

Students from European and American societies might participate vociferously and enthusiastically in class discussions, unafraid to challenge instructors and argue about issues. In contrast, students from Asian societies (e.g., Japan) might exhibit quieter classroom behavior and be less likely to interrupt, challenge the instructor, or pose questions.

Students from some cultures might not want attention drawn to themselves as individuals. Although they might know answers to questions posed by instructors during class, they may be unlikely to volunteer answers during lectures or in class discussions and might not enjoy being praised by an instructor in front of their peers.

Finally, elements of Ogbu's (1987; 1997; Ogbu & Davis, 2003) "resistance culture," or ambivalence or resistance to academic success may be exhibited by students if they perceive themselves as not being a member of or at odds with the dominant culture represented by the institution of higher education, the instructor, or the larger society. According to Ogbu, resistance culture may be prevalent in "involuntary minorities" (i.e., from historically colonized groups).

Also, how students and teachers interact with each other can be affected by whether participants come from high power difference or low power difference cultures. For example, students from Asian societies (higher power difference) might find it less comfortable to interact with professors on a first name or informal basis, which might be common in many U.S. institutions of higher education. This difference in familiarity has also been conceptualized as a difference in horizontal versus vertical cultures and communication styles (Suinn, 2011; Yamauchi & Tharp, 1995).

Whether you are teaching students from different cultural backgrounds or you yourself are teaching in a different cultural milieu, your best resources as cultural informants are often your students. When the first author teaches in another cultural context in the Pacific Islands, she tells her students that one of her goals is to learn about the culture and asks them to share with her about their culture. She also asks them to let her know about any possible violations of cultural norms so that she doesn't behave offensively in their cultural contexts.

Without this approach, how would she have ever known that in Samoa it is considered rude to eat and walk at the same time? Or that discussing dating practices as part of development in a psychology class is not considered appropriate in Chuuk, Federated States of Micronesia? Or that knocking on one's desk is a kind of applause in Dortmund, Germany?

Knowing about the cultural backgrounds of your students can provide you with more common ground so that you can relate to them more effectively and be more approachable. It can also help you to structure activities that work, such as capitalizing on the use of collaboration and minimizing individual competition in working with students from collectivist groups. It can help you to better understand the challenges that your students may face in their quest for higher education and even in being a member of your class. And it can help you to admire the efforts that many students put into higher education that you might not otherwise know about.

Stereotype Threat, Imposter Phenomenon, and Microaggressions

Three kinds of experiences that could affect your students as members of ethnic or other non-majority groups in various disciplines or in academia itself are stereotype threat (Aronson & Steel, 2005), imposter phenomenon (Ewing, Richardson, James-Myer & Russell, 1996; Suinn, 2011), and microaggressions (Suarez-Orozco, Casanova, Martin, Katsiaficas, Cuellar, Smith, & Dias, 2015).

With stereotype threat, a student might feel anxious about possibly authenticating a negative stereotype. For example, a student from a non-majority group might fear that by not doing well, his performance would support negative academic expectations associated with his group, or a person might simply feel doomed to fail. Such threats can also occur in relationship to gender in highly gendered courses of study (e.g., the female in engineering, the male in nursing) and other characteristics (e.g., an attractive woman not expected to do well in math or physics). Anxiety can result in the push to overachieve (to show the stereotype is wrong) or sometimes to give up.

The second concept that can be useful to consider in dealing with students is the imposter phenomenon (Clance & Imes, 1978), or the feeling that one does not really deserve one's success. This can also be affected by what Suinn (2011) has described as "the specter of presumption of special privilege through affirmative action" (p. 164). This can happen among first-generation college students (and new college instructors, too).

A third area of research that is helpful to be aware of is current research on microaggressions (MAs) in higher education (Suarez-Orozco, Casanova, Martin, Katsiaficas, Cuellar, Smith, & Dias, 2015). "Microagressions are 'brief and commonplace daily verbal, behavioral, or environmental indignities, whether intentional or unintentional, that communicate hostile, derogatory, or negative . . . slights and insults' (Sue, Capodilupo, Torino, Bucceri, Holder, Nadal & Esquilin, 2007) toward individuals of underrepresented status" (p. 151). According to these authors, most perpetrators claim to be unaware that their remarks could be taken as hostile, placing the burden of negative interpretation on the victim. These authors point out that there is a cumulative effect of such experiences, and reactions can involve anxiety, depression, and activation of stereotype threat.

Suarez-Orozco and her colleagues (2015) carried out an investigation of MAs in sixty community college classrooms. Their results showed that MAs occurred in close to 30 percent of the classrooms. As the authors summarized, "Although cultural/racial as well as gendered MAs were observed . . . the most frequent types were those that undermined the intelligence and competence of students. MAs were more likely to be delivered on campuses with the highest concentration of minority students and were most frequently delivered by instructors" (Suarez-Orozco et al., 2015, p. 151).

Subtle undermining by instructors who deliver MAs and tolerate student-to-student MAs in classrooms without addressing them can have effects that Suarez-Orozco and her coauthors (2015) compare to "toxic rain." And as many readers who have been subjected to MAs can surely attest, fostering positive learning environments founded on mutual respect is fundamental to learning and promoting the intellectual and personal development of our students.

Race, Racism, and Discrimination

Events in 2010 at the University of California, San Diego (UCSD) illustrate the lingering issue of racism in higher education (Tintocalis, 2010). At that time, fraternity students set up a party that parodied black history month. UCSD administrators responded with a campus-wide teach-in. And in 2013, white students at San Jose State University harassed their black dormitory roommate for weeks (Rivera, 2013). In 2014, racial incidents reported at the University of Mississippi included a noose hung on a statue of a civil rights leader and racial epithets and alcohol thrown at a black student (Valencia & Baldacci, 2014). Aside from obvious examples like this, racism often exists at subtle, even unconscious levels. Furthermore, in complex multicultural societies, racial and cultural dynamics can be subtle and complicated by gender, patterns of immigration, and social status.

It may be erroneous to assume that racism or racial privilege does not exist at your college or university because you believe that you have not experienced it yourself; it may also be erroneous to assume that those of ethnic backgrounds that differ from yours do not experience racism or discrimination or have never done so. As an instructor, you may find it difficult to engage in discussions of these topics with your students, and in some contexts you may believe it to be unnecessary. However, incidents like the one at the USCD or other events in the national media, at your university, or in your community might trigger the need for such a discussion, especially if you teach in the social sciences.

We find it useful to create a safe environment, perhaps by dividing students into pairs or small groups, asking them to discuss personal experiences they have had that involve discrimination, and then asking a few volunteers to share with the larger group. This can be used to lead into a larger, more specific discussion related to racism and discrimination.

Bob Samuels, a lecturer at the University of California, Los Angeles (UCLA) describes how he initiated a discussion with students regarding the UCSD events:

> For the past ten years, I have been trying to get university students to explore their own unconscious cultural racism, and this effort is often stalled by the way people resist learning about uncomfortable aspects of themselves and their culture. For example, when I asked my students at UCLA what they thought about the racist events at UCSD, there was an obvious tension in the classroom, and several students sighed and looked away as if to signal to the other students that we should not enter this uncomfortable subject area. I believe that this type of group passive resistance is a method of social control that students use unconsciously. One of my main strategies to deal with classroom anxiety is to ask students to take out a piece of paper and write down anonymously and quickly what they think the other students are thinking about the current classroom discussion. In making this assignment quick and anonymous, I am trying to get students to not censor themselves, and by having them write about what they think others are thinking, I am able to circumvent some of their defense mechanisms. After I collect students' comments, I then write down some common themes, and I distribute them to the class for an open

> discussion. This process usually starts with nervous laughter, but it often quickly moves to a serious conversation on how people do not want to deal with uncomfortable subjects like racism and the unconscious. What many students tell me is that they have never really dealt with any of these issues in their classes, and while they have taken ethnic studies classes and courses on prejudices, they have never been asked to discuss these issues as they relate to themselves and their fellow students. (Samuels, 2010)

Racism can operate at much more subtle levels in higher education and affect patterns of promotion, hiring, and so on. It is useful for university instructors and personnel to engage in self-examinations of their own possible prejudices: Whom do they expect to do well (or not)? Do any expectations mesh with cultural stereotypes? With whom do they feel comfortable interacting (or not) and why? What are the major cultural or regional stereotypes? How do other factors like gender and regional language variations fit in?

One might also benefit from examining one's approach to the subject being taught. As an example, Armstrong and Wildman (2008) describe the simultaneous difficulties of teaching about race in law courses in a society where "color blindness" is the norm and aspects of white privilege often may be unacknowledged, yet future lawyers must be "prepared to face the racial justice issues that pervade daily life in the United States" (p. 671):

> Discussions about race today occur in an era when the societal notion of colorblindness is a dominant value. The idealized notion of colorblindness tells us that noticing race is wrong because people are equal. The hegemony of colorblindness suggests that by noticing race, one is undermining equality itself. Any conversation about race, or about whiteness in particular, must work against that dominant social norm. (Armstrong & Wildman, 2008, p. 648)

Armstrong and Wildman encourage the inclusion of discussions of racial justice issues, the embedding of personal perspectives in the study of law, and the understanding that legal issues and decisions are couched in decisions affected by race, racial privilege, and culture. They also recommend using readings and films to create shared contexts for discussions, suggestions that apply well to other content areas in addition to law.

SEXUAL ORIENTATION AND GENDER IDENTIFICATION

Sexual orientation and gender identification are also aspects of diversity and include heterosexual, gay, lesbian, bisexual, intersex, and transgender students. Sexual orientation—heterosexual, lesbian, gay, or bisexual—does not include gender identification. Other students may be transgender (i.e., identify with a gender that differs from their biological gender at birth) or intersex (i.e., have atypical sexual characteristics).

We mention these characteristics because students from non-majority groups with respect to sexual orientation and gender identity are likely to have faced (or continue to face) additional challenges in identity formation, such as having been bullied, and they may not experience full acceptance even at the college level. Students from these groups are at higher risk for depression and suicide (Fitzpatrick, Euton, Jones, & Schmidt, 2005; Hong, Espelage, & Kral, 2011), a not insignificant concern since one of the leading causes of death in the United States for the fifteen- to thirty-four-year-old age group was suicide in 2009 (Heron, 2012). For example, in a highly publicized incident in 2010 at Rutgers University, a gay student committed suicide after his roommate videotaped him having a sexual encounter.

In terms of transgender identity development, it is useful to be aware that "Transgender youth have the challenge of integrating a complex gender identity with their personal characteristics, family circumstances, and cultural and ethnic backgrounds (Grossman & D'Angelli, 2006). Such individuals also must reconcile their gender identity with gender expectations of their biologic sex" (Stieglitz, 2010, p. 197). In addition to these developmental challenges, transgender students are likely to have experienced bullying, are at higher risk for suicide, may experience rejection from the lesbian/gay/bisexual community, and have a lack of role models (Grossman & D'Angelli, 2006; Stieglitz, 2010). Stieglitz also mentions that the bulk of research related to transgender issues focuses on risks such as those mentioned here, not the positive aspects of strength and resilience that transgender students also exhibit.

Creating a climate of acceptance at the university starts in all contexts, including the courses that you teach and in the respectful and accepting manner that you exercise with all students. It is also helpful to know that your campus will have a center, office, or organization that can provide resources for students from non-majority sexual orientation and gender identification groups and for faculty members wanting further information.

GENDER

In addition to other areas of diversity, you might notice that the majority of your students are female, which corresponds with current trends among college students. Currently, women outnumber men in college (Goldin, Katz, & Kuziemko, 2006). Given these trends, are there specific ways that gender affects learning?

The first might be by representation in various fields. Despite gains in the 1990s, Costello (2012) found that in the community colleges, women's participation in science, technology, engineering, and math (STEM) courses has declined, and fewer women are graduating in those fields. Costello (2012) and Moughari, Gunn-Wright, and Gault (2012) point out that more jobs are projected in STEM fields and that 80 percent of females graduate from community colleges with majors related to traditionally low-paying jobs, such as those in the social sciences, whereas males comprise 80 percent of majors in STEM fields, with projected higher earnings.

This difference is important because, according to Costello (2012), "Some of the fastest growing occupations in the U.S. economy are in STEM fields with total employment predicted to increase at a considerably faster rate than the job market as a whole" (p. iv). She also mentions that women who graduate from community colleges earn about 77 percent of their male counterparts' salaries, and women hold only about 24 percent of STEM jobs. Efforts to increase women's participation and success in these areas include scholarships, child care, support services, and additional preparatory coursework.

In addition to representation, one might ask if there are "gendered" ways of learning. Several authors have developed theories of learning that relate to gender. For example, Gilligan (1982) developed a theory based upon the idea that women are more caring and learn in ways that are consonant with that characteristic.

Instead of looking for gendered learning styles, we believe that Linda Sax's (2009) approach to college student learning is more valuable for our teaching. Her large-scale, nationwide investigation of how college affects men and women addressed the following concerns:

> Rather than viewing the gender gap in college solely in terms of a zero-sum admissions game, we ought to consider the role that gender plays once students are enrolled. Does gender influence the way that students experience college? Do men and women benefit equally from their engagement with the campus environment? Do interactions with peers and faculty have the same consequences for both genders? Are women and men affected in the same ways by their membership in student clubs, participation in sports, or exposure to racial, ethnic, or cultural diversity? (p. 2)

She found that women, who are typically pressured to remain near home when selecting colleges, do not benefit as much as those whose emotional health and confidence are enhanced by moving away. Women reported more interactions with faculty—and more affirmative ones.

She reports, however, that the effects of these interactions were different for males and females. Specifically, interactions with faculty resulted in more political activism but more strongly for men. Positive interactions with faculty were more tied to positive self-esteem for women and negative self-esteem if the interaction was negative. However, males were less affected by the content of the interaction. Males who had frequent contact with faculty whom they experienced as encouraging reported less traditional beliefs about gender and women's roles in the family. The reverse was true for women. As Sax (2009) explained:

> Instructors need to understand that even when they believe that they are treating men and women the same—and in fact, they might actually be doing so—women and men tend to react differently to these encounters. Particular attention should be paid to the fact that dismissive faculty comments can have a negative effect on female students' academic confidence and even physical well-being. (p. 6)

Furthermore, women appeared to value academic achievement more and spend more time in academic involvement, such as studying, beginning in high school and continuing in college. In college, males are more likely to report being bored. So, according to Sax, when men are academically engaged and study harder, they are influenced more in terms of improvements in confidence and thinking skills. Similarly, exposure to aspects of diversity appear to be more "liberalizing, motivating, and awakening for men than for women" (Sax, 2009, p. 8).

Finally, in interpreting these differences, we echo Sax's (2009) major point: "The reality is that both genders face obstacles and challenges in their pursuit of higher education, and it is incumbent on the higher education community to gain a deeper understanding of the nuances and implications of the gender gap in college" (p. 9). Additionally, it appears that we need to be aware of how our positive and negative interactions might impact women and how diversity experiences and encouragement of academic engagement might positively impact men.

DISABILITY

Disability is also a form of diversity. The notion of disability and disability culture has undergone a radical shift in the past fifteen or so years. Previously, a student with a disability was thought of and even described as "handicapped."

Today, there are several linguistic shifts that reflect underlying attitudinal changes in a positive direction. The first is the use of "person first" language. So a person with autism is not described as an autistic person and a person with a learning disability is not described as a learning-disabled person. Instead, you would say "a person with autism" or "a person with a learning disability." Second, the term "handicap" or "handicapped" is generally passé. Third, disability culture has moved toward a more positive model where disability itself can be celebrated as another aspect of individuality that makes people unique.

If you're wondering about some of the more common forms of disability you'll encounter, table 6.1 shows the percentages of the kinds of disabilities identified at two- and four-year colleges in the United States in which students with disabilities were enrolled. With reporting like this, actual numbers may be higher, since not all students with disabilities identify themselves for services.

It is noteworthy that the majority of disabilities (more than 65 percent, according to table 6.1) are actually invisible disabilities (Raue & Lewis, 2011). The more apparent orthopedic and visual disabilities that people commonly associate with the term "disability" are less prevalent. By way of explanation, ADD (attention deficit disorder) and ADHD (attention deficit hyperactivity disorder) are attentional disorders. The general term "learning disability" refers to disorders involving processing language and numerical information. Other invisible disabilities can involve psychological conditions like depression and anxiety or post-traumatic stress disorder (PTSD).

At each college or university, there is an office or unit that handles issues around students with disabilities. At the beginning of a term, you might receive a confidential letter about a student in your class who has been

Table 6.1. Disabilities in Postsecondary Institutions 2008–2009

Disability Type	Percentage
Specific Learning Disabilities	31
ADD or ADHD	18
Mental Illness/Psychological or Psychiatric Condition	15
Health Impairment/Condition including Chronic Disease	11
Mobility Limitation/Orthopedic Impairment	7
Difficulty Hearing	4
Difficulty Seeing	3
Cognitive Difficulties/Intellectual Disability	3
Other	3
Autism Spectrum Disorders	2
Traumatic Brain Injury	2
Difficulty Speaking/Language Impairment	1

Note: Adapted from *Students with Disabilities at Degree-Granting Postsecondary Institutions* (NCES 2011-018) by Raue, K. & Lewis, L. (2011). U.S. Department of Education, National Center for Education Statistics, p. 8. Washington, DC: U.S. Government Printing Office.

identified as having a disability and who requests accommodations for the disability.

For example, a student with dyslexia may require extra time to take a test or a separate monitored testing situation. A student with a sensory disability (e.g., seeing or hearing) might want to be seated toward the front of the room and may require a note taker or someone who can translate into American Sign Language.

Usually the student has been assigned to a counselor who mediates with instructors and others (such as parents). At this point, you may want to contact the counselor to ask if there are other recommendations for accommodating the disability and to invite the student to talk to you personally whenever he or she wishes. Remember that all information surrounding students' disabilities is confidential, so do not single the student out in class or publicly for a discussion, although you can invite the student to stay and talk with you after class. Most of the time, the best resource about how to accommodate the disability is the student.

Another approach that does not single out students with disabilities is to simply announce, as you go over the syllabus, that students who have disabilities that they wish to have accommodated should make an appointment to see you or to talk to you privately after class. Do not ask them to identify themselves during class. Professors are encouraged by their universities to include statements in their syllabi about accommodating students with disabilities.

If a student tells you that he or she has a disability, you may want to encourage them to have it documented if he or she has not already done so. Refer the student to your campus's center for students with disabilities for testing so that he or she might officially qualify for disability services.

What are some ways to accommodate students with disabilities? According Raue and Lewis (2011), during the years 2008 and 2009, some of the most common accommodations made for students with disabilities in postsecondary institutions were extra exam time, note takers, "faculty-provided written course notes or assignments," "adaptive equipment or technologies," readers, "help with learning strategies or study skills," and "alternative exam formats."

Following are some additional suggestions for helping students with specific disabilities to learn effectively. You will find that some suggestions (e.g., for students with attention and learning disabilities) might help the learning of others (such as students with visual and hearing disabilities or students without disabilities). Additionally, you might contact your institution's office for students with disabilities to find out which technological devices/innovations might be helpful, such as reading devices. Technology services might be provided as well as further advice about online services or modifications.

Attention and Learning Disabilities (Including Dyslexia)

These students may have difficulty reading and writing, so you might want to provide extra time for written assignments, allow for proofreading through your university's center for students with disabilities, and perhaps arrange for monitored tests to take place at your office so that extra time can be given to students. Varying the instructional modes or modalities (e.g., visual, auditory, kinesthetic) that you use can be effective (Davis, 1993).

Physical Disabilities

Students with physical limitations might prefer to sit or position wheelchairs so they can participate but their mobility is not constricted. This location could be close to the room's entrance or sometimes near a power source if an electric wheelchair needs to be recharged. It becomes important that your classroom is accessible. It is also important for instructors to recognize that a student's timeliness might be challenging due to late transportation, weather factors, the need to navigate around obstacles on a street, and the like.

Visual and Auditory Disabilities

The student may prefer to be seated close to you or in front so that he or she can see and hear most effectively. Do not use colors that blend in with your whiteboard or blackboard and are difficult for students to see (e.g., blue chalk blends in with a green board and is far less visible than white or yellow chalk. With a whiteboard, a pastel color like yellow is difficult to see). For PowerPoint presentations, use large, sans serif, bold fonts with only a few items per slide. (It is useful to preview and see if you can read your slides from the back of the room before you teach with them even if you do not have students with visual disabilities.)

For lecture or laboratory classes, Davis (1993) has useful suggestions, including opening with a summary of the previous class, verbally describing visual depictions, facing the class when speaking, distributing lists of new words or technical terms, and making readings available in advance. These suggestions are beneficial for all learners, not only those with disabilities.

A Word about Technology

Now that computers and online materials are so central to teaching, you might examine the latest innovations available for people with disabilities. Readers like Kindles and iPads make reading easier by reading text out loud. Dictation software enables students with visual or learning disabilities to dictate papers. Software is available that enables people who cannot use their voices to speak via their iPads (Fox, 2011).

Principles of universal design (ways to make spaces universally accessible to all, including people with disabilities) have inspired suggestions for making Web pages more accessible. This is an important consideration in designing online courses or having Web enhancements for students who have visual or auditory disabilities, difficulties with motor aspects of computer use, or problems with older equipment and less stable Internet connections. Comden and Burgstahler (2012) recommend the following:

- Use a consistent layout throughout the site, with simple backgrounds and clear contrast.
- Create captions for video and transcriptions for audio.
- Use links that provide verbal descriptions and can be read by software that reads screens for those who are blind.
- Employ standard HTML so features do not require specific software and browsers.

For more details about creating graphics and audio aspects, we suggest that you visit sites such as those associated with Comden and Burgstahler's (2012) work or search the Web for "accessible Web design." Many recommendations and software innovations that could be useful for students with disabilities may quickly outpace the suggestions that we delineate in this book, an especially important consideration in designing online courses.

EMOTIONAL AND MENTAL CHALLENGES

To cope with students' emotional or intellectual challenges, you may have to consult with your university's counseling services. Students may confide that they are depressed or under psychological or psychiatric care. They may be victims of abuse, undergoing painful divorces, dealing with the deaths of family members, suffering serious illnesses, or entertaining suicidal thoughts. Under any of these circumstances, it is worthwhile to contact the counseling center and make sure that the student gets appropriate help.

It may also be important to convey to students that although you care for their welfare, you are not trained as a counselor in terms of providing therapies or treatments, but you will help them to find appropriate resources. If there is a hint of possible suicide, it is incumbent to find assistance through the counseling center, police, or paramedics.

Students might be dealing with traumas often associated with late adolescence and young adulthood—breaking up with boyfriends or girlfriends or other kinds of depressions or traumas. To identify these, you might look out for changes in students' usual behavior—lack of self-care, not showing up for class, not doing assignments, excessive concern about school or grades, changes in class participation, and hostility. These characteristics may indicate more serious psychological or psychiatric illnesses. It is also noteworthy that some serious psychiatric disorders manifest themselves first in young adulthood.

With media attention on acts of violence in college campuses, university personnel have recognized the need for educating faculty members about how to deal with students in distress. For example, the University of California, Santa Barbara (2014a), has a "Distressed Students Response Protocol" that describes indicators of concern (e.g., "change in appearance or hygiene," "behavioral or emotional change," "withdrawal," "alcohol or drug abuse," "excessive or inappropriate anger," "bizarre thoughts or behavior," or "decline in academic performance"). One is asked to answer the question, "Is there danger to self or others?" If the answer is yes, then the student needs immediate psychiatric or medical attention, necessitating calling 911 or the coordinator of student mental health services.

If the answer is "no or not sure but I am concerned," phone numbers for counseling services or campus social services are provided. If the answer is "no, but the student is having academic or personal issues," a list of phone numbers for various offices is provided, including those for counseling services, alcohol and drug programs, offices for international students, women's center, and resource center for sexual and gender diversity. We believe that straightforward guidelines such as these are invaluable.

You may wonder how to approach a student who you are concerned about. It's best to be nonjudgmental when speaking to a student after class: "I've noticed that you haven't been in class lately (or haven't been participating, or haven't been turning in work, etc.), and I am concerned." Sometimes you may find that a student has undertaken a new job or a night shift or has another reason that may have nothing to do with difficulties with the course or psychological issues.

If you are faced with an aggressive and potentially violent student, you should follow guidelines posted by your institution. Again, the University of California, Santa Barbara (2014b), has a useful set of guidelines. We paraphrase them as follows: Determine if you feel safe. If not, you are instructed to "remove yourself from the situation and call 911" or "remain in an open area, preferably with an exit door near you."

If possible, explain which behaviors are acceptable or not. Maintain calmness and tell the student to do so as well if he or she is becoming loud. You might tell the student to make an appointment with you when he or she is calmer. UCSB guidelines suggest debriefing with a colleague and provide a list of other possible contacts, including counseling services, dean of students, and so forth. We also recommend that you document students' unusual behavior and conflicts they may have with you.

Here are some closing thoughts about students with disabilities. Ann Ito, director of the Kokua office at the University of Hawai'i, which serves students with disabilities, has offered the following suggestions for faculty members who deal with students with disabilities (personal communication, April 28, 2012):

- Students with disabilities are qualified; they have met the same admissions standards as other students.
- Every college campus has a service provider or program for students with disabilities that can be a valuable resource.
- Students with disabilities are as diverse as other students.
- Disability information is confidential. Treat it as such. Do not make announcements regarding individual students with disabilities in front of other students or whole classes.

MILITARY SERVICE AND VETERAN STATUS

Military service and veteran status are topics that have received more attention in higher education of late (e.g., Lighthall, 2012), and it is beneficial for college instructors to consider some of the factors associated with this group. Lighthall's (2012) article entitled "Ten Things You Should Know about Today's Student Veteran," provides a useful introduction.

As she explains, veterans are an extremely diverse group—"a rainbow of colors, shapes, religions, sexual orientation, and political views" (Lighthall, 2012, p. 83). Even within that wide range of diversity, it helps to remember that veterans also have a broad array of experiences. Differences in kinds of service, experience in combat and non-combat positions, and so forth can result in military personnel not necessarily having strong feelings of identification with other veterans. Also, veterans have a variety of reasons for pursuing higher education.

However, the transition to higher education can be challenging. As Lighthall (2012) explains,

> The transition from the intensity of military life to a more self-sufficient civilian life can be overwhelming. In some ways, it's similar to the experiences of laid-off workers: both groups may feel disoriented and suffer losses of identity and work-related friendships. But former military personnel report feeling not just disoriented, but deeply alienated from the rest of America; not just sad over the loss of friendships but devastated over the loss of brothers and sisters: not just a temporary destabilizing of identity but a complete identity crisis. . . .
>
> Some veterans hope college will ease their discomfort. . . . On top of the usual student fears, they may also have a spouse or young family to care for and support. They may have new cognitive difficulties or fears of being sin-

> gled out because they fought in an unpopular war. A supportive and informed faculty, therefore, is the key to these veterans' success. (pp. 81–82)

In addition to these points, Lighthall points out that veterans may feel alone on campus, not identifying with the concerns of much younger college students. Some, who have been exposed to explosions, might not know about their own "mild traumatic brain injuries" that manifest in attention and reasoning difficulties. She also explains, "combat trauma is an injury, not a mental illness" and that even if such students are associated with a resulting label (e.g., PTSD), they should be treated "with what traumatic brain injury expert Dr. (and Colonel) Heidi Terrio calls, 'the expectation of recovery'" (Lighthall, 2012, p. 88).

It is the first author's experience that even other faculty members can express harmful stereotypes regarding veterans and active military. Whether faculty agree or disagree with particular military interventions, our role is to support all students' learning and development in respectful and intellectually safe environments.

MOTIVATION

Motivation can be approached in two ways. One is looking at the general motives your students might have for being in your class and how those motives affect their learning. A second aspect to motivation is looking at how motivated your students are in your course and how you might capitalize on what interests them.

General motivation for college can be affected by the reasons your students are in college and are enrolled in your course. According to research by Newstead, Franklyn-Stokes, and Armstead (1996), "The main reasons for entering higher education were to get a good job and to develop useful skills (i.e., means to an end), followed by reasons related to personal development and rather less frequently cited stopgap reasons" (Hoskins & Newstead, 2009, p. 31).

Parental and Peer Pressure

Many students may be undecided about why they are in college and uncertain about what their career goals might be. Going to college is simply the next step after high school graduation, and one follows along with one's peers, experiencing dormitory life, registering for and attending classes. Such a student might have registered for your course because it is required, it had openings, or it fit into a particular time slot. Although these might not be ideal student motives from an instructor's perspective, many college instructors can remember courses that they have taken with similar motives that they truly benefited from.

Of course, you hope to spark interest in and fascination for your subject among all students, but sometimes you may find yourself realistically assessing a student's incentives and recognizing that not every student is going to major in whatever you teach. Sometimes it's important to explain to students why aspects of your content might be of interest to non-majors, and it might be helpful to them in other aspects of their lives, such as psychology for personal growth and later family development or principles of business for managing individual finances. In effect, the benefits of learning about your field that might seem so obvious and undeniable to you might not be as apparent to your students.

Intrinsic and Extrinsic Motivations

Some students have the inner drive and interest in your course that makes them want to learn as much as possible. Other students may be more extrinsically motivated and confess they're taking your course "because it's required" or "for a grade." Woolfolk (2016) points out that intrinsic and extrinsic motives are seldom dichotomous. Students may show elements of both in a single course.

A wise instructor may add references to current events, to students' interests, or to popular culture to add intrinsic interest. Wise instructors are also aware that praise, points, and opportunities to work in groups can be powerful rewards that enhance extrinsic motives, especially when a student is just beginning a new skill, such as practicing a dance step or using conversational French.

Attributions

How students create explanations for their successes or failures or make attributions is central to motivation. Three aspects of attribution theory (Weiner, 1985; 1986; 1992) are stability, controllability, and internal/external locus. These dimensions can be summarized by addressing the following questions:

- Is the cause stable or unstable? Examples of stable causes include always studying hard (or not studying), having a hard professor, being a good (or bad) student. Unstable causes could include not studying for a particular test, not feeling well, preparing extra hard.
- Is the cause internal or external? Internal causes exist inside the person, including not feeling well, studying hard or not so hard for a particular exam, being good or not good at something.

- Is the cause controllable or not controllable? Controllable causes are usually related to the amount of effort one puts in, such as working hard at a project or not spending much time on it. Uncontrollable causes include not being liked by a professor, taking a difficult course, being sick, being distracted by others, or being lucky.

Thinking about students' attributions can be helpful when dealing with individuals who are having difficulty with course material. Helping to move them from unproductive attributions (e.g., "I've never been good at math") to more productive, effort-oriented, and controllable approaches (e.g., "I have to study harder, join a study group, enlist a tutor") can be useful for their success in your course and in college.

Self-Efficacy

Another way to think about students' motivations regarding learning is to consider their self-efficacy related to being a student or in relationship to their studying in specific fields. According to Bandura (1997) and Schunk, Pintrich, and Meece (2008) the following are four sources of self-efficacy: mastery experiences (failures or successes); vicarious experiences (learning from a model, perhaps an instructor or another student); social persuasion (learning from others that one is good at something); and physiological arousal (positive excitement or fear and worry associated with learning). An instructor who provides students with positive mastery experiences, using meaningful praise when truly merited, and who facilitates positive experiences with class work can increase students' self-efficacy, thereby increasing their desire to learn.

CONCLUSION

This overview of student characteristics is intended to provide a starting point for your understanding of your students and for considering how you might adjust your teaching to better serve them. As we have mentioned, there are also on-campus resources (e.g., counseling center, office for students with disabilities) that you may find useful. It can be helpful to familiarize yourself with these offices in advance, either by finding them on the Internet or visiting them in person.

Chapter Seven

Teaching Online

Distance education has gained momentum during the past twenty-five years or so, and online instruction is now an accepted form of instruction, as well as an acceptable way to earn a degree. Furthermore, as universities push their faculty members to become more entrepreneurial, online and distance education programs often fulfill that goal.

With the increasing popularity of online courses, an important question is: Are online learning experiences effective for students? This question appears analogous to instructional media comparisons that have emerged over the years, comparing one form of instructional media to another to see which is best.

In general, we believe that Mayer's (2011) and Clark's (2001) arguments that instructional media comparisons can be fruitless also apply to online instructional tools and techniques. In other words, we believe that one can instruct well or poorly online (as well as face-to-face) depending upon the instructional methods used and the instructor's efforts and expertise, which render the tools themselves nearly meaningless.

We agree with Mayer (2011) that the more important question is about "which instructional methods best foster learning rather than on instructional technology, per se" (p. 442). Keeping these points in mind, we move to a discussion of how you can teach effectively online.

ONLINE TEACHING AND YOU

You may have taken an online class as a student, an experience that can be good preparation for teaching online. As you consider your own future as a professor, you might consider adding online teaching to your repertoire of instructional skills. Thus you might want to know what's involved in planning and teaching an online course. What guidelines are effective for online course design?

You might have heard that teaching online is a great deal of work, especially up-front. That's true, but it's also true that once you have developed a course you can reuse parts of it, like a template for future classes. And you can teach from anywhere—while at a conference in another part of the world or from your own desk at home without having to commute to the office! Finally, online teaching experience—or the willingness to teach online—can enhance your marketability in many fields, so it's worthwhile to develop this aspect of your teaching repertoire.

The first part of this chapter provides an overview of aspects of teaching online that you should consider in preparing to teach online for the first time. The second part of the chapter discusses specific aspects of course development, or decisions you'll need to make in the actual planning of an online course.

Many of the same skills that are involved in good face-to-face teaching can be transferred to online teaching, but an online teaching skill set is different and can involve more written feedback to students, some technology skills, and a great deal of advance planning. Instead of providing a template for an online course or recommendations for specific technology tools (which could become outdated quickly, given the speed of technological innovation), we provide principles for helping you to design such a course effectively.

PREPLANNING: PREPARING TO TEACH ONLINE FOR THE FIRST TIME

1. Set aside sufficient time. Plan in advance and set aside a block of time, at least several weeks, to develop an online course. Be aware that most online courses need to be completely planned out in advance, with all materials prepared and ready for use. If you have a technology assistant (or technologically adept student or willing colleague) who can help you with the technology side, this is far better than working alone. It will save you much time in the end.

2. Examine other courses. Take a look at other online courses in your discipline that are considered by students and colleagues to be good examples. If your university has a unit that assists faculty with teaching and/or technology, ask if they can recommend some courses for you to examine or instructors to consult. You might find techniques worth borrowing. Find what worked well. If you do not have access to good examples from your institution, search the Web for free online courses, such as those listed at www.openculture.com/freeonlinecourses. You might also search online for

syllabi and other materials for online courses at other institutions that are similar to the course you're planning to teach.

3. Determine students' technology proficiency and access. Ascertain (don't assume) your students' general level of proficiency with the technologies you plan to use and the extent to which they have access to technology. Often students have higher levels of proficiency with technologies than their professors do and can be good resources to help you.

On the other hand, don't overestimate your students' previous experiences with online learning. The first author assumed that her students were all experienced with online courses since they were adept with other technologies (like their cell phones) and was surprised to find that several of them needed basic assistance with accessing the class. Further, determine whether your students have consistent and good Internet access. If some students are in rural or developing regions, their level of access to the Internet and ability to use some tools might be limited and different from what you experience at your higher education institution. To effectively reach all students, find out in advance.

4. Assess your own technology skills. Be realistic about your own level of technological proficiency and determine how technology rich your initial online course might be. Perhaps you only want to implement several features that you feel comfortable with in an initial course and adopt more elements in future online course offerings as you gain expertise.

5. Choose your first online course carefully. The best first course to teach online is one that you know well. The initial course the first author taught online was an introductory level educational psychology course that she had taught numerous times. Because she knew the content well and could anticipate the areas that students would find easy or difficult and because she thought ahead about how to translate many of her instructional activities into an online format, she was able to create her first online course rather quickly over several weeks (with the help of an adept technology assistant).

MACRO-LEVEL PLANNING: DECISIONS ABOUT COURSE STRUCTURE

In teaching a traditional face-to-face course, your major decisions about structuring the class might involve whether to deliver lectures or whether to include discussions or small group work. If you're teaching a large introductory class in an auditorium, your choice of a lecture style might be dictated by that circumstance. In deciding to teach online, you'll be faced with many options about how to structure your class and deliver instruction, and it is best to think them all through in advance. Below we provide major decisions you'll have to make, and advantages and disadvantages associated with different solutions.

Will Your Course Be Synchronous, Asynchronous, or Some Combination of Both?

Synchronous Type

In a *synchronous class*, you'll all meet at the same time, together, online at a predetermined time.

Advantage: A major advantage is that your course can be scheduled for a certain block of time, following the regular class schedule, just like a face-to-face class. Since you and your students are used to following this schedule, it can be beneficial in terms of keeping everybody on track, especially for your initial online teaching experiences.

Disadvantages: A major disadvantage is that if your department or higher education institution does not schedule the course in its regular course schedule (e.g., Wednesdays, 3:30–6:00 p.m.), students might register for other face-to-face courses or make work and other commitments that conflict with the times that you hope to hold synchronous meetings (Adam Tanners, personal communication, September 27, 2013). The solution is, of course, to make sure it is scheduled.

Another possible disadvantage to this approach is that if you, as the instructor, have a technical problem, valuable class time can be lost for everyone. To illustrate, the first author went to a conference at a major business hotel in California. She expected to have excellent Internet connectivity via Wi-Fi but found that although her students could communicate with each other, she was unable to effectively communicate with them. As a result, much of the class time for that session was lost. Further, technical problems can sometimes affect a student or a group of students during a synchronous session, causing time to be lost troubleshooting.

A final disadvantage is when a whole-class synchronous meeting does not have a specific purpose and ends up as a general, non-course-related chat session. Thus, there should be some specific goal or task to be accomplished, rather than a general chat session.

Asynchronous Type

In an *asynchronous* class, students are able to access the course at their leisure.

Advantages: This is a good approach if you are teaching people who work full time and can do coursework when they have the time to do so or who are in different time zones. It's also a good approach if your students have limited Internet access and can do work only when they can access computer labs or other facilities. For example, this can be significant if you are teaching students in developing regions or others who would not be expected to have their own computers at home.

Disadvantage: A possible disadvantage to this approach is that it requires students to be highly self-motivated in order to keep up with course materials and due dates. As one student explained to his professor when queried about his lack of course participation, "I sometimes forget that I have an online class."

Dual Type

Of course, you could combine the synchronous and asynchronous approaches. For example, you might have some synchronous meetings initially to make sure that everyone is familiar with the technology, gets to know you and the other participants, and understands how the class will be run. Additionally, you might want to schedule synchronous student presentations, projects, or performances during sessions at the end of a course.

Will Your Course Be Fully Online or a Hybrid?

Fully Online

With a fully online course, you are unlikely to ever meet your students in person, and the entire course is conducted online.

Advantages: The advantages are those connected with the convenience of teaching online and accessing your course from almost anywhere at any time.

Disadvantages: The disadvantages can include less group cohesion and individual responsibility, if you do not work hard to integrate these features into your course. Students may also be less engaged if they are not accustomed to learning online or, again, if you do not work hard to encourage high levels of individual involvement.

Hybrid Type

With a hybrid course, you might meet with students face-to-face at some predetermined points, but some or much of the coursework is done online. For example, when teaching a hybrid course on research methods in psychology to students in American Samoa, the first author traveled there and spent three intensive days meeting with students as a group, familiarizing them with the technology, and providing initial lectures about important concepts in research methods. The rest of the course was taught completely online.

Advantages: The face-to-face meetings provide the kind of social cement and group responsibility that you want to achieve in a class. If you decide to incorporate some face-to-face meetings, make sure they are mandatory. Also, if you haven't taught online before, this is a good intermediate step before teaching completely online.

Disadvantage: You have to go where the students are, or the students have to come to you, which may not be feasible, especially if you are teaching students in different locations.

How Will You Structure the Course in Terms of Assignments?

In other words, will you have regular weekly assignments, or modules, or larger units that need to be completed by certain dates?

Advantage of Weekly Assignments Following a Regular Course Schedule: Students and faculty members are used to this schedule, thus, it is easier to remember to stay on track.

Disadvantage of Weekly Assignments Following a Regular Course Schedule: You might find yourself responding to many threads and posts on a weekly basis, rather than to larger portions of student work as would be the case with units or modules, described below.

Advantages of Modules or Units: Many professors like the modular or unit-based approach because larger assignments can be due at other times and dates than what the typical weekly academic calendar might dictate. For example, you might have a larger unit due several weeks into the semester.

Disadvantages of Modules or Units: The longer the amount of time that elapses between assignments, the easier it is for students and their instructor to get offtrack, so make sure you require periodic assignments. A solution recommended by Adam Tanners (personal communication, September 27, 2013) is a combination of larger units with projects and activities due along with lessons for each week.

TECHNOLOGY AND OTHER PRACTICAL DECISIONS

Which Learning Management System (LMS) Will You Adopt and Which Technology Tools Will You Use?

Most universities adopt an LMS or system of software used for online instruction. Popular examples include Moodle and Blackboard. Most of these include a basic Web page for the class and the following elements: syllabus area, schedule area, profiles (of both students and instructors) or links to individual Web pages, whiteboard, discussion spaces, forums devoted to different topics, chat rooms, resource areas (PDFs of materials and links to other materials are placed here), an assignment tool for submitting work, testing modules, gradebooks, calendar, and mail tools.

It is advisable to use the system that your university adopts rather than trying to find technology tools on your own. Your university is likely to provide technology support for the LMS, and it will be easier for you to learn because others already know it and can consult with you about it. Students are also more likely to be familiar with it, minimizing the time you spend training students on technology use and troubleshooting technology issues.

Further, you might start out by using only a few of the tools, perhaps the easier ones, then integrate other tools into your teaching as you gain experience. Your technology support person is likely to be the best source of information about which tools to adopt for your initial course.

Finally, your university's LMS is likely designed or selected to maintain students' privacy in ensuring their work, personal information, and grades are not publicly available and in violation of the Federal Educational Rights and Privacy Act (FERPA), "a federal law that protects the privacy of students' education records" (U.S. Department of Education, 2015).

Make sure that your online resources meet current accessibility requirements for students with disabilities. Your university should have an office to help with accessibility issues for students with disabilities, and your technology center should be able to assist you with this as well.

How Will You Determine Deadlines for Assigned Work?

Though this might seem so obvious that it doesn't bear mentioning, you'll need to decide how and when you'll accept work from students. What is the cutoff date for the work (e.g., midnight on Tuesdays)? Is that a "hard" deadline, meaning that you will not accept late work? Or will you set your LMS system so that work can't be accepted after a certain time on a certain day?

How Will You Conduct Office Hours and Communicate with Students?

Some instructors create separate e-mail accounts for individual classes. Conducting office hours over an Internet telephone program like Skype (or others) works quite well. The first author found it useful to have a separate Skype account for her class, which she used during office hours and when talking to students.

Similarly, you need to decide whether students should use a university e-mail address (preferred), or another professional e-mail address that they create for the class (that is easily traceable to their individual names so that you'll know who is responding, rather than e-mail addresses that have no connection to students' name and are difficult for you to associate with individual persons).

INSTRUCTIONAL DECISIONS

We prefer to adopt Wiggins & McTighe's (1998) backward planning approach to instruction that we described in chapter 2, rather than what these authors would refer to as an "activity planner's" approach. An activity planner might think, "I have to teach an introductory statistics course. I wonder what activities and experiences will help my students learn?" Instead, backward planning involves determining what the final products or outcomes of learning should be before determining what instructional techniques should be used to facilitate that learning.

From a backward planning perspective, an instructor might consider, "When students have completed my course, what should learning look like? What will they be able to do? How should they be able to demonstrate their learning?" For example, should they be able to implement particular therapy techniques with clients? Should they conduct an oral conversation in Mandarin? Only then might the instructor consider what instructional experiences he or she might implement online to best help students learn.

As you can see, the backward planning approach is inextricably attached to assessment of learning and to learning goals or objectives, some of which may be provided for you by your department, institution, or accrediting agency (and are discussed separately in chapter 2).

The basic elements of planning an online course are similar to those involved in planning any other course, except that one needs to think through and write down, often in narrative form, each aspect of the course. For example, if an instructor has scheduled a discussion on a particular topic for a face-to-face class, she or he might briefly describe orally what she or he expects from the discussion and start off the discussion by putting some leading questions on the board. If the discussion goes offtrack or needs to be moved along in some way, the instructor can pose further questions orally. In an online discussion, the instructor may need to post parameters beforehand, telling students what constitutes an adequate contribution to the discussion (perhaps a paragraph-long statement that includes a well-conceptualized idea and that ties conceptually to other students' posts in a thread).

Once you have decided what learning should look like, you can consider what effective instructional techniques and learning objects to employ within the framework of the particular LMS you are using. Below are further questions to guide your planning.

How Will You Deliver Instruction or Facilitate Learning for Students?

You have numerous options for ways to "deliver instruction" or "facilitate student learning," depending upon the approach that best suits you, your students, and your content. Here are a few examples.

Prerecorded Lectures

If you have a propensity to lecture, this may be the option you select. Prerecorded lectures also have the advantage of being available to students to review multiple times, if they need to—also an advantage for some students with disabilities.

However, take a look at the most engaging online instructors on some of the more popular, freely available online courses. You'll find that these lecturers are quite dynamic, including live demonstrations of physics principles, for example. It's challenging to maintain this level of dynamism in a recorded lecture. Also, it's very difficult to record a whole lecture without multiple takes, and if you are a perfectionist, you might end up rerecording yourself for hours.

Lectures and Discussions Synchronously Delivered, Mini-Lectures and Films

This might be an improvement, since you can insert questions for discussion, ask people to "raise hands" using tools, or answer questions throughout the lecture, and you can pause and call on students or break your class down into smaller discussion groups in various chat rooms where they discuss topics further.

Mini-lectures can be shorter versions of prerecorded lectures, often recorded on YouTube. An advantage is that they are short, and students may not lose interest in the same way that they might with a longer lecture. Another advantage is that if you do multiple "takes" of your lecture, it's easier to redo a shorter lecture. A brief introduction about yourself and the course via shared media Web sites like YouTube is a fine way to begin an online course.

Films and other multimedia presentations that you find online can also be included as instructional tools (again, making sure that copyright restrictions are not violated for classroom or online course use). For example, for an introductory psychology course, an instructor found several useful clips on a shared social media Web site, including short films showing classic experiments.

If you are really enthusiastic about the possibilities of technology, you might teach a class in an online virtual environment like Second Life. If you do not want to teach completely in a virtual environment, you may want to use virtual tools for various topics, like a virtual cadaver for a physiology class.

As for written and other related materials, a benefit of teaching online is that so many resources are available for use in the course. You can provide PDFs of research articles, links to other Web sites, and references to other materials. Most universities have online journals and growing numbers of books in online libraries that can be fine sources of readings for the class.

In examining the list above, you probably already have a strong intuitive sense of which techniques would have engaged you as a student and which would have contributed to rapidly deteriorating wakefulness, especially if you were studying at home with family members and others around, a television on, a cell phone nearby, and nobody checking to see if you have multiple windows open or are also checking your e-mail.

What Kinds of Assignments Will You Require?

You can require many of the same sorts of assignments that you would in a face-to-face class—essays and other written products, discussions, multiple-choice tests, individual and group projects, and even performances. You can employ instructional games or educational group games. For example, an online instructor created business scenarios in which teams worked together to solve economic problems.

Will Your Course Involve Collaboration among Participants?

Opportunities to collaborate and interact will contribute a great deal to the success of your online course—a point demonstrated in distance education research as early as 1994 (Zhang & Fulford, 1994). According to Slavin (2011b), many of the researched cooperative learning techniques involved shared rewards for improvements (e.g., students are divided into groups, where they take baseline quizzes, and then, through a series of quizzes or contests, individual improvement scores are added up to contribute to a group score).

Why does cooperative learning work? According to Robert Slavin (2011b), widely regarded as an expert in cooperative learning,

> Provision of group goals based on the individual learning of all group members may affect cognitive processes directly, by motivating students to engage in peer modeling, cognitive elaboration, and/or practice with one another. Group goals may also lead to group cohesiveness, increasing care and concern among group members and making them feel responsible for one another's achievement. . . . Group goals may motivate students to take responsibility for one another independently of the teacher, thereby solving important classroom

> organization problems and providing increased opportunities for cognitively appropriate learning activities. (p. 352)

All of these positive things can happen in an online environment, as well, if group work is assigned carefully and formatively assessed at each step of completion of a project and if clear guidelines are set up in advance. Individual contributions to group projects also need to be monitored in order to deter slackers and overly dominant group members.

Many instructors of online courses use variations of group projects and group discussions in online environments that suit their own individual instructional situations quite well. For example, you can assign students to smaller groups and give them weekly assignments to discuss specific topics via the Internet (or other means of their choice), then report back in a posting to a group discussion. Another instructor found that students preferred to work in pairs to minimize logistics of arranging group discussions.

In some classes, instructors assign class members to groups. In others, students might choose to work together in a group because they know each other already, share other classes, or live near each other. They might decide that they prefer to do group work via the phone or face-to-face.

As you gain proficiency in online teaching and develop technological expertise, you'll realize that just about any instructional experience you can create in a face-to-face environment can be replicated online in some fashion.

How Will You Assess Students' Learning?

Assessment is much the same as it would be for a face-to-face class, so all of the assessment techniques described in chapter 5 apply to online learning equally effectively. You can administer the same types of written tests, essays, student presentations, and so on.

An area that Rovai (2000) discusses is test security. He explains that over time and with repeated written assignments, you recognize certain patterns of work and writing from individual students to the extent that you can tell whether writing is really theirs. However, if you still have questions, you can use online software to determine whether plagiarism exists. He also suggests using free proctored exam centers for high-stakes tests in the United States, which may be found through a search of the Consortium of College Testing Centers (National College Testing Association, 2016).

When teaching online, the use of rubrics for assessing projects and contributions to discussions can be very helpful both on the instructor's side for the grading and on the students' side for making instructors' expectations clear. A rubric essentially lays out grading criteria with a verbal description associated with each letter grade or a total number of points earned.

For example, in assessing contributions to discussions, Rovai (2000) mentions the following criteria for an A: "messages are characterized by conciseness, clarity of argument, depth of insight into theoretical issues, originality of treatment, relevancy, and sometimes include unusual insights. Arguments are well-supported. . . . Sometimes includes good questions that stimulate discussion. Frequently responds to questions from others" (p. 148).

Additionally, having students use rubrics in which they rate their own and others' contributions to small group discussions and other assignments done outside of class are ways to ensure that students are adequately contributing to group work (Adam Tanners, September 27, 2013, personal communication).

How Can You Maintain a High Level of Interactivity and Provide Useful Feedback to Students?

Clearly, *you* are central to maintaining and fostering a high level of interactivity and enthusiasm in the class. In addition to fostering collaborative experiences, writing positive, encouraging notes to the group, reminding them in playful and even humorous ways about assignments, and sending them informative notes about events on campus and in the community related to the course can help to keep things moving along in positive and constructive ways. Responding to student work in a timely fashion also maintains a good pace for the class. Many online instructors promise to respond to e-mails within forty-eight hours (or less) of receiving them. All of these elements correspond to maintaining a high degree of interactivity, which according to Zhang and Fulford (1994), is associated with the success of distance education courses.

A question you might have is whether you need to respond to every comment that students post. If you do so, this can become overwhelming. Perhaps you can respond to main points in an entire threaded discussion for a group, to the students who have posted until that point, or to the whole class. Be creative in carrying out the delicate balance of acknowledging work without having to respond to every single post. However, make sure you are judiciously commenting on *all* students' work, not just on the few, more verbal students' work, or you are likely to generate student frustration.

COMMON PROBLEMS WITH ONLINE INSTRUCTION

Teaching via the Internet raises questions of privacy, students' compliance with assignment deadlines, and copyright issues.

Privacy

Who will have access to various course materials? Will your course be publicly available or only available for class members? Generally, there are likely to be some parts, such as your students' grades, that legally must be private. There could be other areas that are private, for example, wherein students ask questions that might not be available to the rest of the class. To prevent potential embarrassment, if you think that you are having a private conversation with a student within your LMS, you might verify whether that is indeed the case.

Copyright Issues

Because online courses store and transmit many original works (text, images, video), there can be numerous copyright issues associated with course content. We therefore suggest some areas to elicit further guidance from your higher education institution:

1. Who owns the rights to use and/or modify your course—the university or you?
2. Who owns students' postings and products of the online course?
3. If your course is public, anyone can download videos or other material from it. (We do not recommend making your course public.)
4. Make sure that you are not violating copyright law in drawing upon outside materials in your online course. (Copyright, fair use, and intellectual property issues are also described in Iding and Thomas, 2015, in chapter 9: Ethical and Legal Issues.) For example, even reproducing links to some materials can be protected by law. Further, because something is free or freely available online does not mean that it is not protected by copyright (this includes videos, photographs, etc.).

Your best resource is your institution's technology transfer office for advice on legal issues related to online courses and what you post. Often university libraries and university library Web sites can be good resources for information on this topic, such as Stanford University Libraries (2016), which provides extensive resources on copyright and fair use.

5. According to Paul McKimmy (personal communication, January 7, 2014), "One effective strategy is to reuse materials that have been released under a Creative Commons license. Such materials are purposefully made with some limited conditions. These conditions include attribution to the author, non-modification, and/or noncommercial use—which are easily satisfied in most online courses. You can also use Creative Commons licenses to make your course materials available to others, see http://creativecommons.org."

Laggards

Students not keeping up with material can be a problem in online classes. Creating predictable and firm deadlines (such as contributions to discussions due midnight every Tuesday) can help create routines. Reminders to students also help.

One instructor found that when teaching a course in which all of the students knew each other, she was able to use a combination of "negative feedback" and "group contingencies" quite effectively. That is, she simply praised the students who had gotten their work done and reminded the class that if everyone submitted all of their work up until that point, there would be no need for an additional exam that had been scheduled. This worked very well and would likely be effective in classes where students are working in collaborative groups.

CONCLUSION

We have not purported to provide an exhaustive step-by-step guide to designing an online course here, but we do hope to have provided a general overview of issues to consider and rudimentary questions that you must address in designing your own online courses. Online searches of various university centers for teaching excellence can also yield helpful general, as well as university-specific, advice. We believe that as technologies improve, online learning and teaching capabilities will increase exponentially. And as your proficiency with online teaching grows, the more valuable you will be as an instructor.

Chapter Eight

Creating and Maintaining a Positive and Constructive Environment

Creating a positive classroom environment from the first day forward is one of the best things that you can do to ensure your class progresses smoothly throughout the entire term. In elementary and secondary teaching, this is referred to as "classroom management." If you believe it is unnecessary to consider classroom management at the college level, you have very likely never taught a college class before.

Consider the following scenarios.

- Helen consistently turns in late work and has many excuses that you do not care to dissect further. You deduct several points for lateness, but do not "make an issue" about this, until you let the class know that there is a firm deadline for a high-stakes, take-home midterm examination. This student turns in her exam the week after it is due. She has yet another excuse.
- Mark argues about his grade on a short paper. He says that the quality of his paper is essentially the same as his neighbor's, yet you have given Mark a B instead of an A.
- Several students spend much of the class session focused on their cell phones. If you approach them, they pull out work-related notes that have nothing to do with the topic the class now is focused on.
- A group of three students sits in the back of the room together each class. They talk to each other, play with their cell phones, occasionally roll their eyes when you talk or make slightly sarcastic comments. When you assign work, they act like they haven't understood the assignments. As the term progresses, other students visibly cringe when one of these students speaks out.

- Whenever you raise a question for the class to discuss, John raises his hand to answer. You want to call on others but the other students have become less likely to respond.
- A student spends most of the class on his laptop. You happen to walk by and notice he is working on a paper for another class.
- A promising student, Martha, starts attending class irregularly and stops participating. She appears bored.
- Students are assigned to small groups of four to complete projects. They work together for several weeks to complete the project. One of the students meets with you after class and tells you that a member of their group has not shown up for group meetings or contributed to their project.
- You initiate a discussion with the whole class about several assigned readings. It appears that students are not keeping up with readings.
- You are teaching an online class and several students sporadically respond to discussion topics that you post.

What's an instructor to do? As a new college instructor, the first author ignored some of these behaviors, hoping that they would dissipate. But like ignoring symptoms of a developing car problem, hoping isn't solving. Today she uses assertively proactive techniques, both on her syllabus and in her introductions to her courses, which work quite well.

Her focus is on creating and maintaining a positive learning environment for all—a goal she is explicit about with students, particularly on the first days of class. Many of the types of problems described above have been minimized or eradicated for at least her last several years of teaching. Her syllabus contains the following statement (one that has been lengthened over the years and is mentioned elsewhere in this book):

> Attendance, Participation, Professionalism, Etc.
> Positive and constructive participation, punctuality, professionalism, and attendance are required. More than two unexcused absences or excessive lateness can result in a lower grade or failure in the course. Please attend class regularly and promptly. We benefit from the input of each class member. If you are going to miss a class, please notify the instructor. Professionalism involves basic courtesy, including no cell phones, texting, or non-course-related computer usage during class. If you are taking notes on a laptop or PDA, please put the top down or PDA aside during class discussions out of basic professional courtesy. If you are having difficulty with an aspect of the course, please let the instructor know, as soon as possible, so we can consider solutions and maintain a positive in-class learning environment for all.

Although many instructors may not require attendance, particularly with large lecture classes, most of our classes consist of less than thirty students. The main purposes of requiring attendance are to prevent students from requesting that material that was covered during their absences to be repeated, to ensure that students keep up with the class, and to be fair to other students when participation in collaborative projects and discussions is required.

To prevent the continual distractions of cell phones and laptops, the above policy restricting their use is adopted. These policies are all framed in a positive, not punitive, way. On the first day of class, the instructor reads through the syllabus with the class, answering questions, and emphasizing important points. In reviewing this particular policy, she emphasizes the professionalism and courtesy aspects and usually jokes that she will not be texting during class, either. During her review of the syllabus, as well as during the rest of the course, she strives to maintain an assertive, professional, yet warm and humorous demeanor.

She emphasizes that if anyone is having trouble at any point with the class, to please come and talk to her as soon as the problem becomes apparent. That way, the class can continue in a positive way for everyone.

She repeats this during the second class meeting, as there is usually some "shopping around," with new students adding the course on the second day. Her announcement is something like, "If you have any trouble with this class, please let me know, as soon as possible, so we can find a solution and maintain a positive learning environment for all. There's nothing more disappointing to a professor than finding out at the end of a semester that a student had a problem or issue that we could have solved earlier in the semester." She also mentions, "We've all been in a class before where one person drags the class down in a negative way. This is not going to be that class—we're together for a semester, and let's keep this a positive experience for everyone." Over the past several years, she has had no problems with individuals or small groups "dragging the class down."

She asks students to introduce themselves—describing where they are from, which program they are in, and what their hobbies are. These introductions serve the dual purpose of creating a positive social environment but also helping students become comfortable with speaking in class. After the introductions and at the end of class she states, "I really enjoyed meeting all of you. As you can tell, we have lots of talent in the room. I'm looking forward to the rest of the semester." At the end of each class session, she dismisses the class with "Have a great week. I'll look forward to seeing you again next week."

CONCEPTS FROM BEHAVIORISM

There are several concepts that are useful for instructors at any level to remember—and they come straight from behaviorism.

Classical conditioning involves learning through associations—remember Pavlov and his dog (let's call him Fido) that salivated when a bell was rung? Fido associated the bell with the presentation of food. We also learn via associations—the reader can recall a favorite class or teacher or the least favorite ones. Similarly, college instructors can create positive, respectful, and productive learning environments. Some readers might question whether this is necessary. After all, it's higher education. In our experience, a bit of effort, early on, in terms of creating a positive learning environment is a good investment in preventing negative situations from developing later.

Some readers might also remember learning about operant conditioning (and B. F. Skinner) in an introductory psychology course. Let's review a couple of concepts that can prove helpful even in higher education. Of course there are rewards—positive reinforcement—aimed at increasing wanted behaviors: studying, completing work, positively contributing in class. Positive reinforcers are usually given to students in the form of praise or grades. But here's a concept that instructors could use more frequently and very effectively: negative reinforcement. Negative reinforcers are rewards, too, but they involve the removal of an unpleasant stimulus. For example, "If you finish all of your problems, there won't be a homework assignment," "If everyone participates in the discussion, there won't be a quiz next week," or "If everyone keeps up with readings and does well in discussions and group presentations, I see no need for a sit-down final exam—the take-home exam will be sufficient." Building a few extra assignments into the schedule can be a good way to anticipate making use of negative reinforcement during a term.

Punishment involves reducing unwanted behaviors: cheating, not participating, and so forth. At the higher education level, most "punishments" involve receiving lower grades, fewer points, and so on.

A final concept that can be helpful is praising a student or group that is on task instead of verbally drawing attention to the group or person who is not. Again, if this is done with warmth and humor, students usually "get it" and their attention shifts back to the class.

SOLUTIONS

Considering some of the hypothetical situations described in the beginning of the chapter, we describe possible solutions or areas to reflect upon in developing solutions.

Late Work

This is one of the most common issues that arise in teaching. The best preventative measure, again, is a clearly stated policy in the syllabus, such as the following: "Only *excused* late work will be accepted up until 1 week after the due date; a grade will be deducted from late work in all but the most exceptional circumstances." In some instances, late work may not be acceptable at all, such as with high-stakes papers and take-home exams. And we do reserve the right to grant exceptions—after all, grandmothers die, students get sick, and other family emergencies happen. However, some students offer repeated, extensive, and potentially suspicious excuses—these we leave to readers to discern, but fairness and consistency should underscore policies.

Arguments about Grades

Again, we encourage readers to have clearly stated grading policies on syllabi. Thus, a student should know from the first day how much each assignment is worth in terms of points or percent of the grade. How final grades are calculated should be transparent and stated on the syllabus.

If a student has a question about a grade, we would always take the question seriously, re-examining the assignment if it's a written one (because there could be an error in grade calculation meriting correction) and explaining to the student why the particular grade was assigned. Given that criteria are specific, and grade calculations are clearly stated on the syllabus, arguments about grades are quite rare.

Students Off-Topic with Cell Phones, Laptops, and So On

In addition to reviewing the policy on the syllabus, students might occasionally need gentle reminders, such as, "Let's all focus on what Carlos [another student] is saying," or "Let's give Carlos our full attention." Sometimes moving around the room in close proximity to the cell phone user or the campus newspaper reader is enough. In some scenarios, it might be worth gently reminding the student during a break or after class.

Students Not Keeping Up with Readings

Are readings required? Do students really have to keep up with readings in order to pass the course? If an expensive textbook is associated with the class, students are unlikely to purchase it unless it's absolutely necessary. Readings should be posted on the schedule section of your syllabus, to be completed on days that they are due. Written reflections, regular quizzes (including those via audience response and clicker systems), and active participation in discussions for credit are all ways to ensure that students keep up with readings.

Students Not Contributing to Group Efforts

In the scenario previously described, the instructor finds out only near the end of a project that a student has not been participating in a group project. Again, such an event can be prevented with clear planning and guidelines set out beforehand for students. Breaking down the planning process for group projects into subgoals with associated due dates is a good preventative measure here. Thus, every group can submit an outline describing what each person is responsible to contribute to the group effort. An instructor's monitoring of group progress throughout the term helps, as would requiring students to submit self- and group evaluations at the end of such a project.

A Student Dominates Discussions

Other students lose interest in participating or abdicate responsibility for answering at all. Simple statements like, "Let's hear from someone from the left-hand side of the room," or "Let's hear from someone who hasn't said anything yet today," are ways to encourage other students to respond.

Students Unresponsive to Instructor-Posed Discussion Questions

Here it's best to make sure you're giving them enough "wait time"—at least five seconds (Rowe, 1974). When observing novice university instructors, we've noted that they sometimes ask questions that subtly indicate the "right answer" and don't give enough time before quickly launching into answers. If an instructor sees that students are actively thinking (and after teaching a few classes one becomes sensitized to students' engagement levels), another approach is to use what Svinicki and McKeachie (2014) and other authors refer to as "think-pair-share" (i.e., ask students to discuss the answer with a person sitting next to them, then have a couple of students report back to the class). Advantages to this approach include unanimous engagement and the motivating aspect of talking with peers.

A Small Group of Students Who Are Hostile

It's important to redirect their interactions early, as the whole class can be dragged down. One approach in a small class is to have people work in groups, but have them count off, one through three or four, and meet with all of the other people with the same number. This breaks up the group. Another approach that we see as necessary is to meet with them after class. Tell them that you've noticed that they don't seem engaged in class and ask what can be done to maintain a positive learning environment for all, since you'll be together for the whole semester. You might find out that there is something you can change about your teaching. You might also find out that they could be expressing frustration—that they are required to take your class but don't see that it's necessary given their particular career or degree goals. Here, you can acknowledge that you did not create the degree requirement and brainstorm with them about ways that your subject, though not their major interest, can be useful to them nevertheless.

A Student Stops Participating or Changes Demeanor

Here ask to talk to the student after class or during a break. In our experience, it's invariably something going on outside of class—for example, a divorce, a new job—that's having an impact. You can work with the student to develop a schedule to help him or her finish, or if appropriate, you can refer the student to the counseling center.

Students Participate Sporadically in an Online Class

Here, reminders in the form of encouraging e-mails to the whole class should be helpful. It's also useful to have a few extra assignments built in (e.g., an extra paper, a quiz). You can remind them that the extra assignment will be removed if everyone is up-to-date with readings or contributions to the class. We have also described ways to handle issues related to online teaching in chapter 7.

GENERAL POLICIES

- Treat students respectfully, never resorting to anger or sarcasm. Should you react angrily or sarcastically, you create a hostile "we, the class," versus "you, the instructor," divide.
- Maintain transparency regarding policies and instructional goals—what seems so clear to you might not be so obvious to students. Explain why you have policies and goals.
- Convey an enjoyment of teaching and of your students. Your attitude sets a positive tone, one that can make teaching your class and taking your class a much smoother experience for all.

CONCLUSION

In this chapter, we have provided some tips and guidelines for creating a positive classroom environment. We have shared some typical hypothetical scenarios that can occur and solutions or considerations that could help readers in developing their own solutions. As we stated early in the chapter, a bit of effort in creating a positive and respectful learning environment and in being clear and up front in your syllabus about assignments and grading policies can go a long way in ensuring a positive semester or quarter.

Chapter Nine

University Teaching's Future

In this last chapter, we (a) speculate about the future of university and college teaching and (b) describe the implications such trends might have for higher education professors and instructors. For a summary of trends that include financing in higher education and types of jobs, we direct interested readers to our companion volume, *Becoming a Professor: A Guide to a Career in Higher Education* (Iding & Thomas, 2015).

TRENDS

The issues that we address in the following pages include (a) changing landscape of higher education, (b) instructional techniques and technologies, and (c) student diversity.

Changing Landscape of Higher Education

Due to increased costs associated with higher education and concerns about return on investment, we presume that fields that deliver highly marketable professionals with job prospects available after completion of four-year and two-year degrees will increase or maintain popularity—sciences, technology, engineering, and health care will be among those areas.

Similarly, concerns about immediate marketability and related employment prospects after completing degrees are associated with reduced interest in liberal arts, humanities, and social sciences. Thus, we surmise that fields like literature, history, philosophy, sociology, and psychology will experience lower enrollments, at least in the foreseeable future.

Similarly, we speculate that enrollment in four-year baccalaureate degree programs is likely to drop. A glance at most community college catalogs reveals increased course offerings far beyond basic courses designed to prepare students to transfer to four-year institutions. Less expensive alternatives to universities and four-year colleges, community colleges are likely to continue to experience upsurges both in enrollments and in course offerings. Furthermore, many community colleges offer two-year degrees that enable graduates to be employed immediately, such as in health-related technologies. Also adding to the popularity of community colleges is the trend toward offering baccalaureate degrees at these institutions—an examination of the Community Colleges Baccalaureate Association's (n.d.) listing of such degrees indicates that there are more than one hundred such degrees offered in the United States.

In addition to the decline of the baccalaureate degree as the sine qua non among those aspiring to be college educated, we anticipate that certificate programs and other short-term courses of study offered through community colleges, university extension, and continuing studies programs—both face-to-face and online—will experience dramatic increases.

Such offerings appeal to those newly entering the workforce, others interested in upgrading specific skills and occupation-related capabilities (e.g., technology skills), and those wishing to make career changes. However, a large segment of the population—the retired and those pursuing non-work-related avocations in their free time—can also find such programs valuable, particularly when offered online. For example, the first author of this book completed an online certificate in novel writing through Stanford Continuing Studies—a very rewarding experience, indeed, with some colleagues who were employed and some retired, from locations around the world.

Instructional Techniques and Technologies

We don't anticipate the demise of face-to-face instruction, as some might fear, as there is likely to always be demand and preferences among many for learning in proximity with instructors and classmates. However, with continuing developments in educational psychology, neuropsychology, and learning in higher education and their dissemination among instructors such as our readers, teaching techniques themselves will be upgraded and methods of instruction will change.

Further, technologies will be infused in every aspect of teaching and learning in ways beyond what can be imagined at this writing. For example, online instruction is already commonplace. Thus, we as teachers and our students as learners will have access to learning tools and information that, we hope, will make our educational efforts more expedient and effective.

Student Diversity

As can be surmised from the preceding description of changes in higher education, demographics will continue to evolve. The "traditional college student," usually under age twenty-two, will no longer illustrate what is "typical." By opening the doors to people of different ages, at various points in their careers, and with different purposes for pursuing higher education, what is "typical" will be the myriad faces of diversity. Furthermore, online courses and programs will make higher education programs accessible to those with disabilities and to the geographically distant, dispersed, and isolated, rendering colleges and universities more culturally diverse.

CONCLUSION

The purpose of this chapter has been to suggest trends that are likely to affect the future of teaching in higher education. As the walls of higher education open to many more students of diverse backgrounds and to newer teaching methods, it is our hope that this book has prepared you as a professor or instructor to experiment, to grow in your teaching, to keep up-to-date with new instructional techniques and technologies as they emerge, and, above all, to enjoy the wonderful path you have chosen.

References

AAUP (American Association of University Professors). (1975). *Statement on teaching evaluation.* Retrieved from www.aaup.org/report/statement-teaching-evaluation.

Alexander, P. A. (2006). *Psychology in learning and instruction.* Upper Saddle River, NJ: Pearson.

American Association of Colleges of Nursing (2008). *The essentials of baccalaureate education for professional nursing practice.* Retrieved from www.aacn.nche.edu/education-resources/BaccEssentials08.pdf.

Anderson, L. W., & Krathwohl, D. R. (Eds.). (2001). *A taxonomy for learning, teaching and assessing: A revision of Bloom's taxonomy of educational objectives.* New York: Longman.

Applebee, A. N. (1984). *Contexts for learning to write.* Norwood, NJ: Ablex.

Armstrong, M. J., & Wildman, S. M. (2008). Teaching race/teaching whiteness: Transforming colorblindness to color insight. Santa Clara Univ. Legal Studies Research Paper No. 08-51. *North Carolina Law Review* 86 (635). Retrieved from http://ssrn.com/abstract =1108476.

Aronson, E. (2000). *Nobody left to hate: Teaching compassion after Columbine.* New York: Worth.

Aronson, E., Blaney, N., Stephen, C., Sikes, J., & Snapp, M. (1978). *The jigsaw classroom.* Beverly Hills, CA: Sage.

Aronson, J., & Steele, C. M. (2005). Stereotypes and the fragility of human competence, motivation, and self-concept. In C. Dweck & E. Elliot (Eds.), *Handbook of competence & motivation.* New York: Guilford.

Bandura, A. (1997). *Self-efficacy: The exercise of control.* New York: Freeman.

Bloom, B. S. (1956).*Taxonomy of educational objectives, handbook I: The cognitive domain.* New York: David McKay.

Bloom, B. S., Englehart, M. D., Frost, E. J., Hill, W. H., & Krathwohl, D. R. (1956). *Taxonomy of educational objectives I: Cognitive domain.* New York: David McKay.

Brown, A., & Hughes, I. (2005). Skills and knowledge needs among recent bioscience graduates—How do our courses measure up? *Bioscience Education e-Journal, 6*(2).

Brus, C. P. (2006). Seeking balance in graduate school: A realistic expectation or a dangerous dilemma? *New Directions for Student Services, 2006*(115), 31–45.

Calkins, S., & Micari, M. (2010). Less-than-perfect judges: Evaluating student evaluations. *Thought & Action,* Fall, 7–22.

Catano, V. M., & Harvey, S. (2011). Student perception of teaching effectiveness: Development and validation of the Evaluation of Teaching Competencies Scale (ETCS). *Assessment & Evaluation in Higher Education, 36* (6), 701–17.

Chickering, A. W., & Reisser, L. (1993). *Education and identity* (2nd ed.). San Francisco: Jossey-Bass.

Clance, P. R., & Imes, S. A. (1978). The impostor phenomenon among high achieving women: Dynamics and therapeutic intervention. *Psychotherapy Theory, Research and Practice, 15* (3), 241–47.

Clark, R. C. (2001). *Learning from media: Arguments, analysis, and evidence*. Greenwich, CT: Information Age Publishers.

Comden, D., & Burgstahler, S. (2012). *World wide access: Accessible web design.* Retrieved from www.washington.edu/doit/Brochures/Technology/universal.design.html.

Community Colleges Baccalaureate Association (n.d.). *Baccalaureate conferring locations.* Retrieved from www.accbd.org/resources/baccalaureate-conferring-locations.

Costello, C. B. (2012). *Increasing opportunities for low-income women and student-parents in science, technology, engineering and math at community colleges.* Washington, DC: Institute for Women's Policy Research. Retrieved from www.iwpr.org/initiatives/student-parent-success-initiative/increasing-opportunities-for-low-income-women-and-student-parents-in-science-technology-engineering-and-math-at-community-colleges.

Crook, T. H., & West, R. L. (1990). Name recall performance across the adult life-span. *British Journal of Psychology, 81* (3), 335–49.

Czernochowski, D., Fabiani, M., & Friedman, D. (2008). Use it or lose it? Socio-economic status mitigates age-related decline in a recency/recognition task. *Neurology of Aging, 29,* 945– 58.

Davis, B. G. (1993). *Tools for teaching.* San Francisco: Jossey-Bass.

de Jong, T. (2011). Instruction based on computer simulations. In R. E. Mayer and P. A. Alexander (Eds.), *Handbook of Research on Learning and Instruction* (pp. 446–66). New York: Routledge.

De Jong, T., & van Joolingen, W. R. (2007). Model-facilitated learning. In J. M. Spector, M. D. Merrill, J. J. G. van Merrienboer, & M. P. Driscoll (Eds.), *Handbook of research on educational communication and technology* (3rd ed., pp. 457–68). Hillsdale, NJ: Erlbaum.

Dickens, J., & Arlett, C. (2009). Key aspects of teaching and learning in engineering. In H. Fry, S. Ketteridge, & S. Marshall (Eds.), *A handbook for teaching and learning in higher education: Enhancing academic practice* (3rd ed., pp. 264–81). New York: Routledge.

Dohrer, G. (1991). Do teachers' comments on students' papers help? *College Teaching, 39*(2), 48–54.

Duell, O. K. (1994). Extending wait time and university student achievement. *American Educational Research Journal, 31*(2), 397–414.

Editors' Association of Canada. (2012). *Guidelines for ethical editing of theses/dissertations.* Retrieved from www.editors.ca/hire/theses.html.

Eisenbrey, R. (2010). EPI responds to university presidents on internship regulations. *Economic policy institute: Research and ideas for shared prosperity.* Retrieved from www.epi.org/publication/epi_responds_to_university_presidents_on_internship_regulations.

Elbow, P., & Sorcinelli, M. D. (2011). Using high-stakes and low-stakes writing to enhance learning. In M. Svinicki & W. McKeachie (Eds.), *McKeachie's teaching tips: Strategies, research, and theory for college and university teachers* (13th ed.). Belmont, CA: Wadsworth.

Engelbrecht, P., & Natzel, S. G. (1997). Cultural variations in cognitive style: Field dependence vs. field independence. *School Psychology International, 18*(2), 155–64.

ETS. (2005). *Beyond technical competence: Literacy in information and communication technology.* Retrieved from www.ets.org/Media/Tests/ICT_Literacy/pdf/ICT_Beyond_Technical_Competence.pdf.

Ewing, K., Richardson, T., James-Myer, L., & Russell, R. (1996). The relationship between racial identity attitudes, worldview, and African American graduate students' experience of the imposter phenomenon. *Journal of Black Psychology, 22*, 53–66.

Fabiani, M. (2012). It was the best of times, it was the worst of times: A psychophysiologist's view of cognitive aging. *Psychophysiology, 49,* 283–304. DOI: 10.1111/j.1469-8986.2011.01331.

Feather, A., & Fry, H. (2009). Key aspects of teaching and learning in medicine and dentistry. In H. Fry, S. Ketteridge, & S. Marshall (Eds.), *A handbook for teaching and learning in higher education: Enhancing academic practice* (3rd ed., pp. 424–48). New York: Routledge.

Fitzpatrick, K. K., Euton, S. J., Jones, J. N., & Schmidt, N. B. (2005). Gender role, sexual orientation and suicide risk. *Journal of Affective Disorders, 87*, 35–42.

Fox, Z. (2011, July 25). Four ways iPads are changing the lives of people with disabilities. *Mashable Tech*. Retrieved from http://mashable.com/2011/07/25/ipads-disabilities.

Friesen, N. (2011). The lecture as a transmedial form: A historical analysis. *Educational Researcher, 40*(3), 95–102.

Fulford, C., & Tanare, A. (2011). How to Work a Conference, to Make It Work for You! Five-part series: Part 1: Strategic Conferencing; Part 2: Intro to Slideshow; Part 3: Visuals 101; Part 4: Visuals 102; Part 5: Presentation Delivery. Honolulu, HI: University of Hawaii in conjunction with Association for the Advancement of Computing in Education (AACE). Retrieved from www.youtube.com/playlist?p=PLF0607D1A48F99094.

Gallo, C. (2014). *Talk Like TED: The nine public-speaking secrets of the world's top minds*. New York: St. Martin's Press.

Gardner, H. (1983). *Frames of mind: The theory of multiple intelligences*. New York: Basic Books.

———. (1999). *Intelligence reframed: Multiple intelligences for the 21st century*. New York: Basic Books.

Gilligan, C. (1982). *In a different voice: Psychological theory and women's development*. Cambridge, MA: Harvard University Press.

Goldin, C., Katz, L. F., & Kuziemko, I. (2006). *The homecoming of American college women: The reversal of the college gender gap*. National Bureau of Economic Research, working paper 12139. Retrieved from www.nber.org/papers/w12139.

Graesser, A. C., D'Mello, S. K., & Person, N. (2009). Meta-knowledge in tutoring. In D. J. Hacker, J. Dunlosky, & A. C. Graesser (Eds.), *Metacognition in educational theory and practice*. Mahwah, NJ: Erlbaum.

Gronlund, N. E. (2000). *How to write and use instructional objectives* (6th ed.). Upper Saddle River, NJ: Merrill.

Grossman, A. H., & D'Angelli, A. R. (2006). Transgender youth: Invisible and vulnerable. *Journal of Homosexuality, 51*, 111–28.

Guilford, J. P. (1967). *The nature of human intelligence*. New York: McGraw Hill.

Herba, C., & Phillips, M. (2004). Annotation: Development of facial expression recognition from childhood to adolescence: Behavioural and neurological perspectives. *Journal of Child Psychology and Psychiatry, 45*, 1185–98.

Heron, M. (2012). Deaths: Leading causes for 2009. *National Vital Statistics Report, 61* (7). Retrieved from www.cdc.gov/nchs/data/nvsr/nvsr61/nvsr61_07.pdf.

Hess, F. (2011). Old school: College's most important trend is the rise of the adult student. *The Atlantic*. Retrieved from www.theatlantic.com/business/archive/2011/09/old-school-colleges-most-important-trend-is-the-rise-of-the-adult-student/245823.

Hillocks, G., Jr. (1982). The interaction of instruction, teacher comment and revision in teaching the composing process. *Research in the Teaching of English, 16*(3), 261–78.

———. (1986). *Research on written composition: New directions for teaching*. Urbana, IL: National Conference on Research in English.

Hofstede, G. (1991). *Cultures and organizations: Software of the mind*. London: McGraw-Hill U.K.

———. (2001). *Culture's consequences: Comparing values, behaviors, institutions and organizations across nations*. Thousand Oaks, CA: Sage.

———. (2011). Dimensionalizing cultures: The Hofstede model in context. *Online Readings in Psychology and Culture, Unit 2*. Retrieved from http://scholarworks.gvsu.edu/orpc/vol2/iss1/8.

Hofstede, G. J. (2009). Research on cultures: How to use it in training? *European Journal of Cross-Cultural Competence and Management, 1*(1), 14–21.

Hong, J. S., Espelage, D. L., & Kral, M. J. (2011). Understanding suicide among sexual minority youth in America: An ecological systems analysis. *Journal of Adolescence, 34*, 885–94.

Hoskins, S. L., & Newstead, S. E. (2009). Encouraging student motivation. In H. Fry, S. Ketteridge, & S. Marshall (Eds.), *A handbook for teaching and learning in higher education: Enhancing academic practice* (3rd ed., pp. 27–39). New York: Routledge.

Hughes, I., & Overton, T. (2009). Key aspects of learning and teaching in experimental sciences. In H. Fry, S. Ketteridge, & S. Marshall (Eds.), *A handbook for teaching and learning in higher education: Enhancing academic practice* (3rd ed., pp. 226–45). New York: Routledge.

Iding, M. (1994). Feedback from college composition students: Are teachers' comments useful? *College Student Journal, 28*(3), 330–38.

———. (1997). How analogies foster learning from science texts. *Instructional Science, 25*(4), 233–53.

Iding, M., Crosby, M. E., Auernheimer, B., & Klemm, E. B. (2009). Website credibility: Why do people believe what they believe? *Instructional Science, 37,* 43–63.

Iding, M., & Greene, W. (1995). Peer writing commentary for preservice teachers. *Journal of Professional Studies, 2*(2), 66–74.

Iding, M., & Greene, W. (1997). Guided peer response for preservice teachers: Exercises beyond editing. *Journal of Reading Education, 22*(3), 15–25.

Iding, M., Greene, W., Fukunaga, C., & Ige, J. (1996). Improving preservice teachers' writing response and writing skills through peer response activities. *Journal of Professional Studies, 4*(1), 34–44.

Iding, M., & Thomas, R. M. (2015). *Becoming a professor: A guide to a career in higher education.* Lanham, MD: Rowman & Littlefield.

Johnson, D. W., & Johnson, R. (1985). Classroom conflict: Controversy over debate in learning groups. *American Educational Research Journal, 22,* 237–56.

Johnson, D. W., Johnson, R., & Smith, K. A. (1996). Academic controversy: Enriching college instruction through intellectual conflict. *ASHE-ERIC higher education report, 25*(3). Washington, DC: George Washington University Graduate School of Education and Human Development.

Johnson, R. (2000). The authority of the student evaluations questionnaire. *Teaching in Higher Education, 5,* 419–34.

Kagan, S. (1974). Field dependence and conformity of rural Mexican and urban Anglo-American Children. *Child Development, 45*(3), 765–71.

Khourey-Bowers, C. (2006). Structured academic controversy: A peaceful approach to controversial issues. *The American Biology Teacher, 68*(5). Retrieved from www.nabt.org/websites/institution/File/pdfs/publications/abt/2006/068-05-0008.pdf.

King, A. (1993). From sage on the stage to guide on the side. *College Teaching, 41,* 30–35.

Knapper, C. (2001). Broadening our approach to teaching evaluation. *New Directions for Teaching and Learning, 88,* 3–9.

Kraushaar, J. M., & Novak, D. (2010). Examining the effects of student multitasking with laptops during the lecture. *Journal of Information Systems Education, 21*(2), 241–51.

Lambiotte, J., Dansereau, D., O'Donnell, A., Young, M., Skaggs, L., & Hall, R. (1988). Effects of cooperative script manipulations on initial learning and transfer. *Cognition and Instruction, 5,* 103–21.

Lambiotte, J., Dansereau, D., O'Donnell, A., Young, M., Skaggs, L., Hall, R., & Rocklin, T. (1987). Manipulating cooperative scripts for teaching and learning. *Journal of Educational Psychology, 4,* 424–30.

Lighthall, A. (2012). Ten things you should know about today's student veteran. *Thought & Action (28),* 81–90.

Lipka, S. (2010, April 21). U.S. Labor Department releases new rules for "educational" internships. *The Chronicle of Higher Education.* Retrieved from http://chronicle.com/article/US-Labor-Department-Releases/65197.

Mangan, K. (2013, October 4). Inside the flipped classroom. *The Chronicle of Higher Education,* B18–B21.

Mayer, R. E. (1984). Twenty-five years of research on advance organizers. *Instructional Science, 8,* 133–69.

———. (2011). Instruction based on visualizations. In R. E. Mayer & P. A. Alexander (Eds.), *Handbook of research on learning and instruction* (pp. 427–445). New York: Routledge.

Morton, A. (2009). Lecturing to large groups. In H. Fry, S. Ketteridge, & S. Marshall (Eds.), *A handbook for teaching and learning in higher education: Enhancing academic practice* (3rd ed., pp. 58–71). New York: Routledge.

Moughari, L., Gunn-Wright, R., & Gault, B. (2012). Gender segregation in fields of study at community colleges and implications for future earnings. *Institute for women's policy research fact sheet.* Retrieved from www.iwpr.org/publications/pubs/gender-segregation-in-fields-of-study-at-community-colleges-and-implications-for-future-earnings.

Multitasking 101. (2011, May). Stat Watch. *Harvard Business Review,* 4, p. W34.

Naftulin, D., Ware, J., & Donnelly, F. (1973). The Doctor Fox lecture: A paradigm of educational seduction. *Journal of Medical Education, 48*, 630–35.

National Center for Education Statistics. (2016). Fast facts: Enrollment. Retrieved from http://nces.ed.gov/fastfacts/display.asp?id=98.

National College Testing Association. (2016). Consortium of College Testing Centers. Retrieved from www.ncta-testing.org/cctc.

Newstead, S. E., Franklyn-Stokes, A., & Armstead, P. (1996). Individual differences in student cheating. *Journal of Educational Psychology, 88*, 229–41.

Ogbu, J. U. (1987). Variability in minority school performance: A problem in search of an explanation. *Anthropology & Education Quarterly, 18*, 312–34.

———. (1997). Understanding the school performance of urban blacks: Some essential background knowledge. In H. Walberg, O. Reyes, & R. P. Weissburg (Eds.), *Children and youth: Interdisciplinary perspectives* (pp. 190–240). Norwood, NJ: Ablex.

Ogbu, J. U., & Davis, A. (2003). *Black American students in an affluent suburb: A study of academic disengagement.* Mahwah, NJ: Lawrence Erlbaum Publishers.

Perry, W. G., Jr. (1970). *Forms of intellectual and ethical development in the college years: A scheme.* New York: Holt, Rinehart, and Winston.

———. (1981). Cognitive and ethical growth: The making of meaning. In Arthur W. Chickering and associates, *The modern American college* (pp. 76–116). San Francisco: Jossey-Bass.

Rabbitt, P. (1965). An age decrement in the ability to ignore irrelevant information. *Journal of Gerontology, 20*, 233–38.

Raue, K., & Lewis, L. (2011). *Students with disabilities at degree-granting postsecondary institutions.* (NCES 2011-018). U.S. Department of Education, National Center for Education Statistics. Washington, DC: U.S. Government Printing Office.

Rivera, C. (2013, December 1). Race at issue on San Jose campus. *Los Angeles Times*, pp. A37–A38.

Rosenshine, B., & Stevens, R. (1986). Teaching functions. In M. Wittrock (Ed.), *Handbook of research on teaching* (3rd ed, pp. 376–91). New York: Macmillan.

Rovai, A. P. (2000). Online and traditional assessments: What is the difference? *Internet and Higher Education, 3*, 141–51.

Rowe, M. B. (1974). Wait-time and rewards as instructional values: Their influence on language, logic, and fate control. Part 1: Wait-time. *Journal of Research in Science Teaching, 11*, 81–94.

Samuels, B. (2010). Unconscious racism at the University of California. *Huffington Post.* Retrieved from www.huffingtonpost.com/bob-samuels/unconscious-racism-at-the_b_491817.html.

Sax, L. J. (2009). Gender matters: The variable effect of gender on the student experience. *About Campus, 14*(2), 2–10.

Schunk, D. H., Pintrich, P. R., & Meece, J. R. (2008). *Motivation in education: Theory, research, and applications* (3rd ed.). Columbus, OH: Merrill/Prentice Hall.

Slavin, R. E. (2011a). *Educational psychology: Theory and practice* (10th ed.). Boston: Pearson.

———. (2011b). Instruction based on cooperative learning. In R. E. Mayer & P. A. Alexander (Eds.), *Handbook of research on learning and instruction* (pp. 344–60). New York: Routledge.

Sowell, E. R., Thompson, P. M., Holmes, C. J., Jernigan, T. L., & Toga, A. W. (1999, October). In vivo evidence for post-adolescent brain maturation in frontal and striatal regions. *Nature Neuroscience, 2*(10), 859–61.

Spoorem, P., Brocks, B., & Mortelmans, D. (2013). On the validity of student evaluation of teaching: The state of the art. *Review of Educational Research, 83*(4), 598–642.

Spurlin, J. E., Dansereau, D. F., Larson, C. O., & Brooks, L. W. (1984). Cooperative learning strategies in processing descriptive text: Effects of role and activity level of the learner. *Cognition and Instruction, 1*, 451–63.

Stanford University Libraries. (2016). *Copyright & fair use overview*. Retrieved from http://fairuse.stanford.edu.

Sternberg, R. J. (2006). The rainbow project: Enhancing the SAT through assessments of analytical, practical, and creative skills. *Intelligence, 34*, 321–50.

Sternberg, R. J., & Williams, W. M. (2010). *Educational psychology* (2nd ed.). Upper Saddle River, NJ: Merrill.

Stieglitz, K. A. (2010). Development, risk and resilience of transgender youth. *Journal of the Association of Nurses in AIDS Care, 21*(3), 192–206.

Suarez-Orozco, C., Casanova, S., Martin, M., Katsiaficas, D., Cuellar, V., Smith, N. A., & Dias, S. I. (2015). Toxic rain in class: Classroom interpersonal microaggressions. *Educational Researcher, 44*(3), 151–60.

Sue, D. W., Capodilupo, C. M., Torino, G. C., Bucceri, J. M., Holder, A. M. B., Nadal, K. L., & Esquilin, M. (2007). Racial microaggressions in everyday life: Implications for clinical practice. *American Psychologist, 62*(4), 271–86.

Suinn, R. M. (2011). Teaching culturally diverse students. In *McKeachie's teaching tips: Strategies, research, and theory for college and university teachers* (13th ed., pp. 151–70). Belmont, CA: Wadsworth.

Svinicki, M., & McKeachie, W. J. (2014). *McKeachie's teaching tips: Strategies, research, and theory for college and university teachers* (14th ed.). Belmont, CA: Wadsworth.

Sweller, J., & Chandler, P. (1994). Why some material is difficult to learn. *Cognition and Instruction, 12*(3), 185–233.

Thomas, R. G., & Thomas, R. M. (2008). *Effective teaching in correctional settings.* Springfield, IL: Charles C Thomas.

Thurstone, L. L. (1938). *Primary mental abilities.* Chicago: University of Chicago Press.

Tintocalis, A. (2010). UCSD students say deeper racism exists on campus. *KBPS News.* Retrieved from www.kpbs.org/news/2010/feb/24/ucsd-students-say-deeper-racism-exists-campus.

Toga, A. W., Thompson, P. M., & Sowell, E. R. (2006). Mapping brain maturation. *Trends in Neurosciences, 29*(3), 148–59.

Tufte, E. R. (2006). *The cognitive style of PowerPoint: Pitching out corrupts within* (2nd ed.). Cheshire, CT: Graphics Press.

University of California, Santa Barbara. (2014a). *Distressed students response protocol.* Retrieved from www.sa.ucsb.edu/responding-to-distressed-students/protocol.

———. (2014b). *Responding to distressed students: Aggression and potential violence.* Retrieved from www.sa.ucsb.edu/responding-to-distressed-students/concerns/demanding-aggressive/aggression-potential-violence.

University of Central Florida. (2008). *Program assessment handbook: Guidelines for planning and implementing quality enhancing efforts.* Retrieved from http://oeas.ucf.edu/doc/acad_assess_handbook.pdf.

University of Hawai'i Office of Institutional Equity. (2016). *Sample Title IX syllabus template.* Retrieved from www.hawaii.edu/titleix/files/2016/08/07-13-16-Sample-Title-IX-Syllabus-OIE.pdf.

U.S. Department of Education. (2015). *Family educational rights and privacy act.* Retrieved from www2.ed.gov/policy/gen/guid/fpco/ferpa/index.html.

U.S. Department of Labor Wage and Hour Division. (2010). Internship programs under the fair labor standards board. *Fact Sheet #71.* Retrieved from www.dol.gov/whd/regs/compliance/whdfs71.pdf.

Valencia, N., & Baldacci, M. (2014, February 22). Ole Miss racial incidents have many feeling uneasy. CNN. Retrieved from www.cnn.com/2014/02/21/us/mississippi-meredith-statue/index.html?iref=allsearch.

Waugh, K. C., & Gronlund, N. E. (2013). *Assessment of student achievement* (10th ed.). Upper Saddle River, NJ: Pearson.

Weiner, B. (1985). An attributional theory of achievement motivation and emotion. *Psychological Review*, 92, 548–73.

———. (1986). *An attributional theory of motivation and emotion*. New York: Springer-Verlag.

———. (1992). *Human motivation: Metaphors, theories and research*. Newbury Park, CA: Sage.

Wiggins, G., & McTighe, J. (1998). *Understanding by design*. Alexandria, VA: Association for Supervision and Curriculum Design.

Wilson, R. C. (1986). Improving faculty teaching: Effective use of student evaluations and consultation. *Journal of Higher Education, 57*, 196–211.

Witkin, H. A., Moore, C. A., Goodenough, D. R., & Cox, P. W. (1977). Field-dependent and field-independent cognitive styles and their educational implications. *Review of Educational Research, 47*(1), 1–64.

Woolfolk, A. (2016). *Educational psychology* (13th ed.). New York: Pearson.

Yamauchi, L., & Tharp, R. (1995). Culturally compatible conversations in Native American classrooms. *Linguistics and Education, 74*, 349–67.

Yurgelun-Todd, D. (2007). Emotional and cognitive changes during adolescence. *Current Opinion in Neurobiology, 17*, 251–57.

Zellermayer, M. (1989). The study of teachers' written feedback to students' writing: Changes in theoretical considerations and the expansion of research contexts. *Instructional Science, 18*, 145–65.

Zhang, S., & Fulford, C. P. (1994). Are interaction time and psychological interactivity the same thing in the distance learning television classroom? *Educational Technology, 34*(6), 58–64.

Zhou, D. (2005, September 19). College textbook prices are unfair and unnecessary. *Christian Science Monitor*. Retrieved from www.csmonitor.com/2005/0919/p09s02-coop.html.

Ziv, N. (1984). The effect of teacher comment on the writing of four college freshmen. In R. Beach & L. Bridwell (Eds.), *New directions in composition research*. New York: Guilford Press.

About the Authors

Marie K. Iding (PhD, University of California, Santa Barbara) is a professor of educational psychology at the University of Hawai'i at Mānoa. She has also taught in California, American Samoa, and Chuuk (Federated States of Micronesia). She has written a number of articles regarding various aspects of learning and teaching and has taught and conducted research in the United States, Norway, Singapore, Micronesia, and American Samoa. She has presented her education- and technology-related research at many international venues, including Scotland, Switzerland, Spain, Germany, Kenya, Jamaica, and South Africa and has delivered workshops on publication and teaching in Vietnam, Hawai'i, and Ecuador. She also served as guest researcher in the Department of Information Science and Media Studies at the University of Bergen, Norway, and as visiting professor at the Computational Social Science Laboratory in the Center for Applied Information and Communication Technology (ICT) at Copenhagen Business School, Denmark.

R. Murray Thomas (PhD, Stanford University) was emeritus professor of educational psychology at the University of California, Santa Barbara, where he also directed a program on international education and served as dean of the Gevirtz Graduate School of Education. He began his career as a teacher for Kamehameha Schools and Mid-Pacific Institute in the 1940s, when he also served as crime reporter for *The Honolulu Advertiser* and wrote press releases for University of Hawai'i at Mānoa's School of Tropical Agriculture. He has taught and conducted cultural research in American Samoa, Indonesia, and the United States. His professional publications exceed four hundred, including sixty books for which he served as author, coauthor, or editor.